# In Fear of her Life

The True Story of a Violent Marriage

MAVERICK HOUSE PUBLISHERS

Published by Maverick House,
Main Street, Dunshaughlin, Co. Meath, Ireland
info@maverickhouse.com
http://www.maverickhouse.com

ISBN 1-905379-04-8

This edition 2006

5 4 3 2

*The paper used in this book comes from wood pulp of managed forests. For every tree felled, at least one tree is planted, thereby renewing natural resources.*

The moral rights of the authors have been asserted

A CIP catalogue record for this book is available from the British Library.

## NOTE

The names of the characters in this story have been changed to protect Frances Smith, who is also writing under a false name. The facts in the story are sadly true, however.

# Acknowledgments

I would like to thank my family and friends who have stood by me over the years, in particular my four daughters. I wouldn't be here if it were not for them. Thanks to my father, who will always hold a special place in my heart.

Thanks to Michael Kealey and Fiona Barry of William Fry solicitors for reading the manuscript.

I would also like to thank my Mediterranean friend, and, of course, Erin McCafferty who wrote my story.

Frances Smith

# PART ONE

*chapter one*

HAVE YOU EVER been punched in the stomach? Ever had someone draw back their fist and aim their knuckles at the soft wad of flesh on the lower part of your body?

Do you know how it feels to have a pain shooting through your insides? Through the flesh like a knife; a pain so bad you think you're going to die. You feel like puking but you can't. Your heart is beating as if it's going to burst out of you and you can't see straight. The world is just a blur—a blur of pain.

Lying on the cold tiles of the hall floor, I was staring up at the ceiling as the pain coursed through my body. All I could make out was the crystal chandelier above me. It was one of two he'd stolen.

"Came off the back of a lorry," he told me. Of course, I knew otherwise but they brightened up the otherwise dreary hall of the two-bedroom council house we lived in.

Now I was looking at it from a different perspective—little shards of crystal, twinkling like stars, catching the light and reflecting streams of rainbow.

I remember thinking for some reason that it looked beautiful. It's funny the thoughts that occur to you when you think you are dying. I'd never looked at it like that before.

It occurred to me then as I lay in a pool of blood on the floor that there were many things I had yet to see, yet to do, yet to say.

Now it was too late.

"This is the end of my life," I thought. Part of me was grateful.

Despite the pain, a feeling of serenity washed over me. For the first time in many years I felt happy.

"Get up off the floor you ugly bitch."

I could hear his voice booming and through the blur I could make out his face leaning over me. Weathered from years of drinking, his skin had the rosy-hue of an alcoholic. His lip twitched in disgust. His wild, bloodshot eyes were full of anger and contempt.

He ran his hand though his greasy hair that had once been the colour of coal but was now greying prematurely and leaned over me.

I caught the stench of his breath. It reeked of booze and the smell turned my stomach and made me want to retch.

"Do you hear me? Get up," he shouted. "Get off that fucking floor."

He clenched his teeth in anger. I wanted to move but the pain was too bad. I searched his face, pleading with my eyes for him to stop. Where was the real Johnny Smith?

It was no good; I couldn't find him. He was lost in an alcoholic haze.

Then he kicked me. His size 10 boot with the steel-capped toe came straight at me. I thought he was aiming for my eyes and that I'd be blinded for life but no, he aimed lower down, into the soft, vulnerable flesh of my breast—the same breast that had fed his four children; the same breast he once lovingly fondled. I blacked out.

I don't know how long I lay on that floor. Maybe I was there for hours, maybe days. It seemed like a lifetime. When I did come to my first feeling was of regret. I was alive but I wanted to be dead. Then I felt angry.

"God," I thought "Why have you done this to me? Why have you brought me back for more? What have I done to deserve this? Let me die God, please let me die," I prayed.

But no, God was having none of it.

"Ma," I heard a familiar voice scream.

"Ma, are you alright? Jesus, Holy Mary and Joseph. What has he done to you now Ma?" Aoife, my 18-year-old daughter was standing over me.

I could see the look of fear on her face now—fear mixed with anger.

"That fucking bastard. How could he do this to you and you after coming from the hospital?"

It was true. I'd been released from hospital just two days before, after a serious operation on my bowels. I still had the stitches in my stomach but I knew from the amount of blood and pus oozing out of me that they had burst.

The tears rolled down Aoife's face but she pushed them away with her hand as she bent down and stroked my head. Her voice was high pitched and panicked.

"Don't worry Ma. He's gone now Ma, I'll call an ambulance."

"No! Not an ambulance."

I couldn't bear to go back to the hospital. The thought of strangers staring at me in shock and disbelief; the sympathetic looks from the nurses; the questions from the doctors and the abject shame.

"No Aoife," I whispered and there was determination in my voice.

"No way. I'm not going back to the hospital."

"But you need a doctor Ma. Look at you Ma, you're a mess."

She was upset and annoyed at me for not complying, but she knew I hated hospitals. I'd been in and out of them for years.

She gave in.

"Alright Ma but we're going to the doctor. Mark's outside in the car. He'll bring us Ma."

Somehow I got into the car with the help of Aoife and her boyfriend Mark. They supported me as I limped towards the passenger seat. The pain was excruciating and I screamed out loud as I got in.

Mark drove us to the local GP. He knew what had happened but he was mortified; he didn't know where to look.

"Is she alright Aoife?" I heard him say. "I know he's your Da, but he's an animal. I can't believe he did that to her," he shook his head in disgust.

Even the doctor was shocked.

"Jesus Frances," she said when she saw my undressed body—the burst stitches on my stomach, the cuts on my breast and the dark blue bruises, which were all over my body like maps.

"What in the name of God happened to you?"

I said nothing at first.

"I ran into a door, I fell down the stairs, I was mugged by a young fella on the street," all the usual excuses ran through my head like wild fire.

For years I'd been covering up for him. It was like a kneejerk reaction.

"Tell nobody," I'd think to myself. "Pretend it didn't happen."

Jesus, I almost convinced myself half the time. But this time was different. Something inside me snapped that day. I looked her in the eye and took a deep breath.

"It was Johnny Smith," I said, "My husband."

*chapter two*

I WASN'T ALWAYS a battered wife. At one stage I was a carefree child who held her head high when she walked down the street.

I was brought up in the heart of Dublin. Most of my childhood memories revolve around the inner city and looking back it wasn't a bad place to live. It was dirty and rundown, but it had a strong community atmosphere and we loved it as children.

Both my parents were born and bred Dubliners. They met and married when my mother was just 19 and my father 20. Their first home was a flat in a tenement building. We lived in a small two-bedroom, corporation flat. Our flat was on a second storey. It had concrete steps leading up to it and a small balcony outside with railings. There was an enclosed

13

yard in front of the flats where we used to play as children.

There were six kids in the Reilly household. All of us children slept in one bedroom and my parents in the other. Anthony or Anto as we called him, was the eldest child. He was six years older than me. Then came Helen who was four years my elder. I had three younger sisters—Sorcha, Patricia and Fiona, who was born seven years after Patricia—she was an afterthought as they say.

There was barely enough room for all of us to live in the flat but my father was a worker with an average salary and it took all his earnings to pay the rent and put food on the table. As a child I never thought of our family as poor but looking back I realise now that times were hard. It was the 70s in Dublin and everyone was "pulling the devil by the tail".

Mind you we always had enough to eat; my father made sure of that, but there was no money for anything extra. We wore the same clothes day in day out and we had no toys.

Looking back, however, most of the children in the area were poor and we spent our days hanging around the streets. We hung around in gangs.

The streets were our playground and we knew every nook and cranny in the local area. There were no trees and no patches of greenery to play in. Instead we made do with the concrete and the rubble, the burnt out cars and the washing lines. We used to make swings from the poles where the women hung their clothes and play hide and seek in the pram shed belonging to the flats. That was where the street traders stored the carts, which during the day held their goods.

When we got a bit older we ventured further afield and ran around the traders with their colourful stalls that lined the pavements. They sold everything from fruit and vegetables to toilet rolls. Most had been traders for generations and everyone was a Dublin character. They'd shout at us when we knocked the apples or toppled bars of chocolate off their carts.

We'd laugh and run like the wind back home where we'd sit on the steps of the flat and play games.

We used to look forward to Da coming back from the pub on a Saturday evening. He wasn't a heavy drinker but he liked a few jars with the other men after a long week of working. He'd bring us sweets. Our favourites were Lucky numbers—chocolate numbers wrapped in shiny, coloured wrappers.

I remember looking up at him coming in the hall door with the brown paper bag tucked under his arm and a big smile on his otherwise sad face.

"Here you are, children," he'd say, as he poured the contents of the bag onto the kitchen table.

"Go on pick your favourite number".

We'd shriek with joy and make a grab for our favourite number. I always wanted six. Believe me nothing ever tasted quite as good as those lucky numbers. How little it takes to satisfy a child.

Although I have some good memories of my childhood in general it was an unhappy one.

I was smaller than average and very slight growing up. I had long, black, straight hair and small eyes. People said I had a winning smile but I never thought of myself as good looking. My father however used to say I was the prettiest girl on the street. Of course I didn't believe him. I'd get embarrassed and blush.

"Da," I'd say. "You're only embarrassing me. Would you give over!"

Then he'd laugh. I loved it when he laughed; he didn't do it often enough. He'd look so sad sometimes it would break my heart.

He was a kind and gentle man who wouldn't hurt a fly. In all the years I've known him I've never seen my father raise his hand to another living soul and he rarely shouted or got angry.

He enjoyed the odd pint and he'd often put a bet on a horse at the weekend. He used to get us to cheer the horse on, in front of the television. In general however he was a moderate man who craved a simple life. He came from a respectable family who had worked in Dublin Castle. My mother's family were street traders and considered to be a step below his. All of us children took after our father. None of us were like my Ma who was hard as nails.

Looking back I think my father just wasn't able for her. She was the boss in the house and the complete opposite of him in both temperament and appearance. She was tall and dark; he on the other hand was at least a head smaller than her and very fair.

I can quite honestly say that I lived in fear of my mother—we all did. She was a severe woman with a terrible temper who blatantly resented her children and she seemed to have no feelings.

I never once remember her showing me any sign of affection. She never hugged me or kissed me; she never told me that she loved me and she never gave me any encouragement. She didn't even mark our birthdays. We had no money for parties but I never once received a present or a card or even just a "Happy Birthday" and a hug.

My mother treated all of us in the same manner except for Fiona the youngest—who for some reason she held a soft spot for. I remember her playing with Fiona when she was just a little baby. That was something she never did with us.

My father arrived home with a red anorak for me when I was six-years old. It was wintertime and I had nothing warm to wear. It was one that he'd made himself in his workshop. I was over the moon.

"Oh, thanks a million, Da," I jumped up and down with excitement and he grinned. My father loved to make us happy in anyway he could.

My mother walked into the room with a face on her like thunder.

"What the hell is that?" she turned to my father. "What did you buy her that for?"

My poor father never even got a chance to explain. The angry woman grabbed the coat out of my hands before I could even try it on.

"You won't be needing this young Frances," she said, as she threw it into the roaring fire.

I cried myself to sleep that night. I wasn't crying for the anorak. I was crying for the mad temper that my mother possessed. I realise now she was jealous of the relationship I had with my father. She was a possessive woman and she hated the fact that he loved me so much.

My mother seemed to have no guilt about any of her actions. Ironically she was a strict Catholic and she drummed religion into us from an early age. She used to march us all to mass on a Sunday morning and make us pray in the evenings. She used to get up at six o'clock to attend morning mass in the local convent each day. In that respect she was a product of her upbringing. Her own mother was a devout Catholic.

My mother didn't talk about her childhood but we all knew my grandmother, her mother, as another severe woman and I can only imagine how she raised her children.

At one stage when she was in hospital, three of us were sent to Goldenbridge Orphanage. I was five-years-old at the time. Helen, my sister, was nine and Anto was eleven. Although we spent only three weeks in the place, they were three long weeks and the memories of Goldenbridge are ingrained in my mind.

My mother had pneumonia at the time and my father had the task of looking after the three of us. I think it was too much for the poor man. He was out at work during the day and there was no one to mind us when we returned from school. He was too proud to ask for assistance from our relatives.

He decided it would be no harm to place his three eldest children in the care of the Mercy nuns. It was meant to be a temporary situation and he planned to bring us home after a few weeks when my mother had made a full recovery.

To this day my father denies we were ever in Goldenbridge. I think he has blocked it out of his memory. But I remember clearly walking down the street holding on to his hand with Helen on his other side and Anto skipping along beside us.

We didn't know my mother had pneumonia then, we were told she was in hospital having another baby.

It was a sunny day and my father had told us we were going to the seaside. I was excited but I knew something wasn't quite right. It's funny the things children pick up on. My father looked worried.

Eventually we reached an imposing looking building. To a child it seemed huge. We walked through the gates and a shiver ran down my spine.

The nuns greeted us and we had to sit in what looked like a hall while one of them took our details. I was standing by my father's side as he sat on a big chair in front of a desk. An old nun with a wrinkled face and a croaky voice was writing in a big leather-bound book. It was the biggest book I had ever seen in my life and I remember how withered her hands looked. I was terrified of the nun and I didn't like the place. It smelt of laundry and burnt food.

I remember the pattern of the tiles on the floor— yellow crosses on big brown squares. There were pictures of the Virgin Mary and crucifixes on the walls. A stained glass window hung above the old nun's head. Suddenly Helen started crying.

"I want to go home, Da," she said to my father.

"We're not going home love. You're going to stay here with your brother and sister for a while. The nuns will look after you and I'll come and get you soon."

That set us all off. Even Anto, who was 11 at the time, was crying. We didn't want to be left in that horrible place and my father knew it. I think it broke his heart to leave us there. He hugged all three of us before leaving and I clung on to his neck with my little hands. He had to tear me away.

"Be a good girl, Frances," he said, as he kissed me on the head and turned to walk off. His footsteps echoed down the corridor as his figure disappeared into the distance. I felt deserted and utterly forlorn.

As soon as he'd gone the nuns turned on us. They'd been charming in his presence but now they were like different people; they were stern and aggressive and we were terrified of them.

Boys and girls were segregated in Goldenbridge so we were separated from Anto immediately. I clung on to Helen as we were escorted to a big dormitory full of other young girls most of whom had been there for years. They all looked underfed and frightened. It's no wonder; the food was horrific and the nuns treated us like animals.

For a five-year-old it was a horrific ordeal and I began to wet the bed at night. There was a laywoman working there who took a dislike to me and the first time it happened she turned on me.

She was a big, stout woman with a hard face and narrow eyes. I'd say she was in her early 20s. Her short, chopped hair and slight moustache on her upper lip gave her a menacing look. I was terrified of her, as were all the girls. We'd hear her heavy step and rush to hide under the bed covers.

That morning she took me by the ear and marched me into the laundry room. It stank of disinfectant and I remember how cold the tiles of the floor were. I was bare foot.

"Wash those sheets, you little brat," she screamed, as she threw me towards a steel bath-like structure where the laundry was done. My head banged off the basin and I fell to the ground.

I was dizzy from the bang on my head but I managed to pull myself up. I began crying pitifully and that just angered her more. Then I tried to wash the sheets but I was so small I couldn't reach into the water.

She grabbed me by the hair and lifted me off the ground with her other hand. I was plunged into the hot, dirty water and she held my head underneath so I couldn't breathe. I flayed around and tried to pull away from her but she was too strong.

I nearly drowned and by the time she let go, I was purple and splattering for air. Since that day I have a phobia of water. I don't even like to be near it and I've never learnt to swim.

Anto was only in the orphanage a few days before he escaped. He came up to us in the yard where we played and whispered to Helen and I that he was going. He planned to jump out the second floor window of the dormitory in the middle of the night.

"Don't worry, I'll come back to get you," he said, as he patted me on the head. That night he ran away. The nuns were furious but there was nothing they could do. We waited and waited for his return but he never came back and eventually we resigned ourselves to a life at Goldenbridge.

After Anto escaped, my father came to visit us one Sunday afternoon. We thought he had come to take us back. We were overjoyed and ran to hug him. He lifted both of us into his arms at the same time and covered our face with kisses.

"Ah, my lovely girls," he smiled. "I've missed you both so much. Have you been good for the nuns, have you?"

He placed us back down on the ground and we nodded at him. The nuns had already warned us not to say a bad word about the orphanage.

"If you do," the sister had said, "there'll be beatings."

That was enough to frighten us into staying silent. We'd already seen what the nuns were capable of doing. They regularly beat many of the other girls in a cruel, sadistic fashion and they often whacked us over the head with their hands.

When my father questioned us about our life in Goldenbridge we acted as if we were happy there. There was a nun standing right beside us at the time listening to make sure we didn't spill the beans.

"Are we going home Da?" I whispered to him when the nun wasn't looking. There were tears in my eyes.

"Soon my love, soon," he promised.

But he didn't take us home and we had to return to the cold dormitory that night crying our little hearts out. He had brought us a cake as a special treat. Of course we never saw it after he left. The nuns took it off him promising to give it to us later. They must have eaten it themselves.

Once more we went to bed cold and hungry, wanting to be home and missing our family and friends. In our innocence we thought we'd done something wrong to be sent to the orphanage, so we blamed ourselves. It wasn't long however until Da returned and took us home. It was like being released from prison.

I couldn't talk about my time in Goldenbridge for years afterwards. I pushed it to the back of my mind and didn't even discuss it with Helen. It was only when, as an adult, I saw a documentary about it that I started to think about my time there and mentioned it to my sister. Neither of us talked about it for years because we felt ashamed. To this day I'm afraid of the dark and I can trace back my first feelings of fear to my time in the orphanage.

Once I was home, however, I put Goldenbridge out of my mind and got on with my life in the inner city. My mother had been released from hospital by the time we returned. She never mentioned Golden-bridge and I honestly don't think that she cared about our suffering there. She was always too wrapped up in herself to worry about us.

*chapter three*

THE ONLY OTHER time I was away from home was
when I was sent to live with my grandmother for a few
months. I was seven-years-old at the time and it was
quite common back then for one child to be farmed
out to a grandparent.

It was my mother's decision for me to go and I
remember my father being unhappy about it, but he
dared not go against her wishes. She was such a strong,
dominant personality. I think she wanted rid of me
even back then. One day she came in and coldly
announced that I was moving. She put the few pieces
of my clothing into a small suitcase and took me by
the hand as we walked down the street. I was crying
but she didn't seem to care.

My grandmother was a tough street trader who lived a ten minute walk away from my family home. Although she was hard as nails she was as devout as my mother. I remember her getting up at five o'clock each morning to be in mass by six before she went to the fruit market. She used to come in to me each night when I was in bed and bless me with holy water before I went to sleep.

On Saturdays I accompanied her to Smithfield fruit market where she bought her stock for the city centre stall. I'd spend the day hawking it with her.

I thought I was great standing at a stall beside her. I'd watch her talk to the customers, lick her lips as she scooped the apples and oranges into a bag and tie them deftly with a knot. She knew everyone in the area and she had regular customers who would always buy their fruit and vegetables from her.

"Get your apples and oranges here," she'd call out in the way only Dublin street traders can. "Five for truppence."

I can still hear her voice in my head. You'd hear it for miles around and it had that hoarseness that comes with years of working on the streets in all weathers. I could never throw my voice the way she could and I didn't have her way of dealing with the customers. I was too shy.

Although I was glad to get away from my mother, I hated living with my grandmother who was just as strict and severe. I missed my brother and my sisters and I wanted to go home. I'll never forget the day my father suddenly appeared at her front door.

"Da," I screamed, as I ran to hug him. "Da, I hate it here. Please Da, can I come home?" I cried.

"Get your suitcase young Frances," he said quietly as he lifted me off the ground and into his arms. "You're coming back with me."

I never found out what was said between my parents but my father obviously had his way in the end.

Looking back now I realise just how strict my mother was. If we broke any of her rules, we were beaten. She used to whack us on the face or over the head with the back of her hand and she often took a belt to us.

On one occasion she turned on my sister Helen who had disobeyed her. My mother had had a fight with my father at the time. He had moved out of the house for a few days and was staying with his sister and we were all forbidden to talk to him.

One day she caught Helen having a conversation with him on the street. She was livid with anger. Poor Helen was only 10-years-old at the time. I remember her arriving in the door of the house that evening.

"There you are, you little brat," my mother screamed at her. "I saw you speaking to your Da today."

"I'm sorry Ma, I'm really sorry," said Helen trying to run past her up the stairs.

"Come here to me," said my mother, and she ran up the stairs after her.

Helen legged it into the bedroom and banged the door behind her. We were already in bed, cowering under the sheets, afraid of what was coming next. There was nothing quite like my mother's temper and we knew it.

The door banged open. Ma walked in, her face full of rage. She had a wire coat hanger in her hand—one that she had purposefully bent open so she could use it as a stick.

"Bend over and lift up your jumper," she screamed at poor Helen. We all started to cry as she proceeded to beat her across the back with the hanger. There was blood on the floor and Helen lay in a heap by the time she had finished.

When we got a bit older we took to sitting around on the steps of the flats. We'd tell ghost stories and gossip about everyone in the neighbourhood. We knew all the neighbours. One of them was an old woman called Granny. We used to call her "Nasty Granny" and we hated her as children. The poor woman was the butt of many a joke and we plagued her by ringing her doorbell and then running away. But then she always seemed to be causing trouble for us. She lived in the flat below ours and she seemed to spend her life looking out the window. She didn't miss a thing.

My brother Anto was short-sighted and had to wear a pair of national health glasses when he was a child; they were plain brown, rimmed glasses and he hated them. He was supposed to wear them all the time but he didn't. He used to leave them on the windowsill of Granny's flat while he was out playing and then put them on before he'd go back into the house so my parents wouldn't know.

Granny used to come out of her house and scream at the top of her voice, "Anto you forgot your glasses! They're here Anto, come and get them."

If anyone in the neighbourhood shouted the whole area heard it. It used to drive him mad because my mother would hear and come running out onto the balcony. She'd force him to wear the glasses.

My mother seemed to spend half her life on that balcony. I can see her now standing there with her hands on her hips, shouting abuse at whoever was on the street below. She always had something to give about.

At the time there was an old man called Fred who was disabled and he used to sit outside the gates of the flat complex. My mother came looking for me one day. I saw her coming and ran past Fred, up the steps and down the other side of the flats. I thought I got away with it.

"Is our Frances there, Fred?" she shouted.

I nearly died when Fred answered her.

"Yes. Mrs. Reilly. She's over the other side with her mates".

I was furious with him for telling her. I knew she'd kill me.

"You see you," I said to Fred when she'd left. "I'll lift you out of it and leave you for dead."

Once I went on the mitch from school. The school phoned to tell my mother but she pretended to know nothing about it when I returned that evening.

"Did you have a nice day at school Frances?" she wanted to know.

"Yes, Ma. It was a good day," I lied.

I had actually spent the day hanging out in the bike shed in the grounds of another school, which wasn't far away. I was thrilled with myself, thinking I'd got away with it.

I nearly died when she marched into the schoolyard the next morning and clobbered me around the head in front of the other pupils.

"Thought you got away with it?" she sneered. "I'll show you, young Frances Reilly!"

I was so embarrassed I didn't dare to do it for a long time after that.

*chapter four*

MY LIFE CHANGED the day I met Johnny Smith. I'll never forget the first time we met. I was 12-years-old and he was all of 15 and a half.

My God, he was gorgeous—all the girls fancied him. He was tall for his age—about 5 foot 6 with a pale complexion and chiselled features. He had straight, jet-black hair, streaked back with Brylcreem.

Johnny always wore the best of clothes and took great care with his appearance. I can see him now in his flares, his well-ironed shirt and his v-neck jumper. He used to a wear a black leather jacket that was too big for him in the shoulders but it gave him an air of authority. His shoes were always perfectly clean.

It was the late 70s and he was a rebel without a cause. There was an air of coolness about him—a presence you might say. Heads turned when Johnny Smith walked into a room.

I'd seen him around and I knew who he was. Johnny's reputation preceded him. He was a tough guy who lived just around the corner from my flat. He was the kind of fella you wouldn't bring home to your mother.

We met for the first time at a teenage disco. I had just started to go to the disco with my sister Patricia. We had to be home by nine o'clock but we looked forward to it all week. Looking back we were very innocent then; we were only children on the verge of adolescence.

Johnny approached me one night outside the disco where we were queuing to get in. It was a lovely, sunny evening and he strode up to me decked out in his finery. My heart skipped a beat when I realised he was walking towards me.

"Have you got a membership card?" he said, looking me straight in the eye and smiling. I could hardly speak with the excitement. Here was Johnny Smith talking to me Frances Reilly. I knew the whole queue was watching us. Somehow I got the words out.

"I do, but I'm not signing you in," I giggled, trying to act cool in front of him. He was head and shoulders above me and I was quaking inside. I'd never had a boyfriend and I didn't know how to talk to strange boys.

"It's not for me, it's for my friend," he said. "Ahh, go on, please?"

He looked at me with those ice-blue eyes of his and smiled, and for a few seconds the world stopped turning. It was the kind of smile that would break your heart in two—all innocent and doe-like. He always killed me with that smile. In the space of a few seconds I was a gibbering mess and I would have done anything he wanted.

I already belonged to Johnny Smith and nothing could tear us apart. Of course, he didn't know that yet and it took some persuasion on his part before I agreed to sign his friend in.

"Was that Johnny Smith?" said June, my best friend, half in awe and half in disapproval. "You'd want to stay away from him. My Ma says he's bad news."

But it was too late. I'd already fallen for the man who would make my life a living hell. Later in the disco he sidled up to me when no one was around.

"Look what I have," he said looking around the run-down function room as he spoke. He produced a handful of coins from his pocket. I panicked. It was just a few pounds but it was more money than I'd ever seen in my life.

"Where on earth did you get that from?"

I was shocked.

"Do you want some money?" he grinned at me, pleased at my reaction.

"I do not," I said, feigning disapproval. "Where did it come from?"

"I got it from the slot machine," said Johnny puffing out his chest and grinning from ear to ear.

There were two poker machines in the disco and he'd obviously been working them that night. I was impressed but I wasn't going to let him know.

"Go away from me," I pushed him away jokingly and laughed. He laughed too. Then he turned and strutted off.

"Sure I'll see you around," he called over his shoulder, catching my eye as he left.

At first we simply hung around together. We were walking down the street one night when Johnny tried to take my hand in his. Jesus, I nearly died on the spot.

"What are you doing?" I pulled my hand away from his. I'd never had a boy hold my hand before and I wasn't sure how to react.

"Sure I'm only trying to hold your hand Frances," he said, kicking the pavement with his foot. Now he was embarrassed. I blushed profusely and that seemed to please him. He lifted his head, looking sheepish and smiled. Then I held my hand out and he grabbed it. We walked down the road like that until two of his mates passed us on their bikes.

"Well look who it is? Johnny Smith, and holding a girl's hand! Are you in love Johnny? Ooh, Johnny's got a girlfriend."

Now we both blushed and the lads thought it hilarious.

"Johnny's in lur-ve, Johnny's in lur-ve," their singsong chorus echoed down the street as they sped off on their bikes.

That was it. The whole neighbourhood knew about us. Johnny Smith fancied me. I was the girl everyone wanted to hang out with. I was cool. I was cooler than cool. I was Johnny Smith's girl.

Johnny had a part-time job but he soon gave that up and became a motorcycle courier for a big company—a job that gave him his own motorbike and completed his already cool persona. I thought I was in heaven. Not only did I have a boyfriend—I had a boyfriend with a bike! I was still in school at the time and he seemed so sophisticated to me. He was a working man—a man of independent means.

We used to ride around on the bike for hours at a time—me on the back, holding on for dear life and him proud as punch, grinning like a Cheshire cat as we sped along. He was supposed to be out delivering packages for the company he worked for but more often than not he was with me.

I used to bunk off school to be with Johnny. I wasn't particularly good in school. I was a bit of a dreamer and didn't apply myself. To me, studying was just a chore and I got out of it whenever I could.

I left school shortly after I met Johnny to look after my mother who suffered from ill health. She used to take to her bed every now and then, for a few days at a time. I now realise she wasn't actually sick but there were times when she just couldn't cope with a family of six young children.

Not long after I left, I got a job in a factory but I didn't last long there. I rarely went in. I would leave the house in the morning, having arranged to meet Johnny around the corner. He'd be there with the bike and the two of us would spend the day driving around while he delivered packages.

We'd stop for lunch in Stephen's Green and feed bread to the ducks. Sometimes we'd take a spin up the Dublin Mountains. We'd take a picnic and come back in the evening. Those were the days. Neither of us had any serious responsibilities and life seemed perfect. We were the best of friends back then. We'd talk about anything and everything and spend the day laughing. Within a few weeks I was head over heels in love with Johnny.

Of course, my family had no idea I was with him. My mother would have hit the roof if she knew. On one occasion he called to the flat to take me out. I nearly died. She was standing on the balcony and she stuck her head over when he beeped his horn.

"Who's that young fella and what does he want?" she said.

I acted like I didn't know who he was. That was the first time she found out I was seeing Johnny Smith. We'd been with each other for months at that stage. She went mad.

"You're to stay away from him," she warned me. "He's nothing but trouble. If I catch you near him, I'll kill you."

Even fear of my mother didn't stop me seeing Johnny. We were already inseparable and the whole neighbourhood knew about us. Everyone knew too that he was violent towards his own mother. Everyone that is, except me. I turned a deaf ear to anything bad I heard about him. I refused to believe that he was anything but perfect.

He came from a large family. Johnny lived with his mother and his younger brother. His father had left years ago and he never talked about him or why his parents had separated.

His mother was a cold woman and he clearly had no respect for her. She lived in one room upstairs in the family home and he and his younger brother shared the other bedroom. They rarely mixed although they lived in the same two-up, two-down house. But Johnny didn't talk about his family and I was wary to ask. I didn't want anything to spoil the easy-going relationship we had.

Back then he was a different person. He didn't drink or smoke but he was a real man's man when the other lads were around. He was a natural leader; he made the decisions in the gang and all the other lads followed.

With me however, he was as gentle as a lamb. He used to joke and slag me off in a light-hearted way and I'd giggle and blush. I'd pretend to be offended but deep down I loved it. And he'd do anything for me too.

Another bonus of being Johnny Smith's girlfriend was the presents he'd buy me. I remember driving around with him on the motorbike and passing by shops. He always had more than enough money. Where it came from I don't know and I didn't question. If I pointed out anything I liked in a shop window Johnny would note it and arrive with it under his arm the next day.

I'll never forget the time he presented me with a full-length dress and matching coat. It cost the earth and I couldn't believe it. I was speechless when I saw the outfit, which had come from an expensive dress shop on Camden Street. The dress was made of wool. It was cream with cocoa brown flowers embroidered across it and there was a matching, three-quarter-length cardigan to go with it. I thought they were the most beautiful clothes I'd ever seen in my life.

I was a petite, little thing back then and they fitted me like a glove. You'd think the outfit had been made for me. I looked gorgeous; at least I thought I did. But I couldn't wear it. I knew my mother would be furious if she found out Johnny had been buying me expensive presents.

So I hid them along with all the other items of clothing he'd bought me—under the bed in a battered old suitcase. I couldn't let my sisters or brother see them either. They'd tell my mother and there would be murder.

It wasn't long however until Johnny noticed I wasn't wearing the dress. A week later he asked why and I had to think quickly. I couldn't tell him that my mother knew nothing about it and that she'd kill me if she did.

"Well, I have no shoes to go with it," I lied. "I can't wear it without the right shoes".

I thought I'd got away with it but the following day he came to collect me.

"Look what I have for you," he grinned from ear to ear as he produced a box wrapped in brown paper. I unwrapped it slowly and found a pair of brown, knee-high boots in my size. They were perfect and I loved them as much as I loved the dress. I thought I was the business.

I tried on the shoes with the whole ensemble that evening and admired my reflection in the mirror. I was 14-years-old at the time but I remember thinking to myself, "Now I'm all grown up."

I thought I looked like a model. I was dying to show the whole outfit to my sisters but of course I couldn't. I swirled around in front of the mirror admiring my reflection. Then suddenly I heard a noise; it was my older sister Helen.

"Jesus Frances, where did you get those from?" she nearly died of a heart attack when she walked into the room.

"Shh," I warned her. "Johnny bought them for me," I said. "Don't tell Ma, she'll go mad."

"I'm telling her," Helen announced defiantly. "She'll murder you!" and before I could bat an eyelid she was thundering down the stairs.

My mother was up those stairs in two shakes of a lambs tail. The bedroom door swung open and she stood in front of me with her hands on her hips.

There was blue murder in my house that night. Chaos! You could hear my screams half way down the road as she beat me with a belt.

Funnily enough she stopped forbidding me to see Johnny after that. I suppose she just had to accept the relationship. Perhaps she realised she couldn't put an end to it and I think even she was secretly impressed by the presents he bought me.

*chapter five*

THE FIRST TIME I slept with Johnny I became pregnant. For years my mother had warned me not to give in to young men. She didn't tell me why. I was left to find out the facts of life from the older girls on the street.

Up until then I had allowed Johnny to kiss me but as he got older he wanted more. He could be very persuasive and eventually I gave in. I was still naïve back then and I certainly didn't associate babies with sexual intercourse. The first time we slept together was in his house one afternoon when his mother was out.

"Come on Frances, please, you know I love you and I'll look after you," he said.

I didn't want to do it. I was 15-years-old and so nervous I felt like crying. But I'd have done anything to keep Johnny happy.

It only happened once but it was enough to make me pregnant. Two weeks later I had missed a period but I wasn't in the least bit worried. Pregnancy didn't even cross my mind.

I was six weeks pregnant when I miscarried and it still hadn't dawned on me that I was going to have a baby. I remember standing outside a shop. I'd arranged to meet Johnny there at seven in the evening. I thought my period had finally come because I was bleeding heavily and I had excruciating pains in my stomach. I was standing on the pavement holding onto my stomach when I met Johnny.

"What's wrong with you Frances?" he questioned.

"I can't walk. I've awful pains in my stomach Johnny". I was doubled over in agony.

He took me on the back of his bike and brought me to his older sister's house. She brought me in, sat me down and made me a cup of tea. After an hour the pain hadn't subsided.

"You should really tell your Ma," she said to me. "I think you might be pregnant."

"I'm not pregnant," I retorted. "And there's no way I'll tell my Ma about the pains," I shook my head defiantly. "She's the last person I'd go to for help."

I could never go to my mother with a problem of any kind.

"Right so," said Johnny's sister. "We've got to get you to a hospital and fast."

I couldn't sit on the bike because the pains were so bad so I had to get the bus to the Coombe hospital. I remember sitting in the back of the bus, clutching my stomach with Johnny by my side. I nearly passed out with the pain. The blood started to trickle down my legs and in no time at all my clothes were soaked. By the time I reached the hospital I could hardly walk but somehow I managed to hobble into the accident and emergency room.

It didn't take long for the doctor to realise I had miscarried. They kept me in overnight because I had lost so much blood. I was very weak and in a state of shock at the time. I hadn't realised I was pregnant and I didn't understand what was happening to my body.

They did a D and C on me and my mother and older brother Anto came to visit. Johnny had phoned them.

"I'll fuckin' kill him," said Anto. He was livid with anger.

"No Anto, don't," I pleaded. "It's my fault too."

I was released from hospital the next day and for a while after that I was very run down. Anto gave Johnny a good talking to, but it didn't do much good. Within a few months I was pregnant again. This time my mother was the first to realise. Even the second time round I didn't know myself. She marched me off

43

to the local doctor for tests and he confirmed her suspicions.

Even when the doctor told me I was going to have a baby it didn't sink in. Part of me was terrified and my way of dealing with the fear was to block it out of my head. I tried not to think about the pregnancy but I knew I had to tell Johnny. He called for me one evening soon after I was diagnosed and we went for a ride on his motorbike. We sped along through the city. It was a cold winter's night and I had a short skirt on. My legs were frozen.

"Are you hungry?" he asked, as he pulled up outside Macari's, the local chipper. I waited outside while he went in and brought out two singles of chips. We stood in the cold eating them or rather he ate, I was too nervous. Eventually he noticed I hadn't touched the chips.

"What's wrong with you? Do you not want those chips?" he asked me.

"Johnny," I said. "Johnny, I've something to tell you."

He looked at me as he picked the hot, greasy chips one-by-one out of the bag. They stank of vinegar. He licked his fingers.

"What's wrong chicken?"

He stared into my eyes and my heart melted. I loved it when he called me 'chicken'. He was so loving back then and I always fell for that particular puppy-dog look.

"What is it?" he said gently.

"Johnny," I was crying now. Big, hot, tears came rolling down my face and fell into the chips.

"Johnny I'm up the pole. I'm pregnant."

He dropped the chips suddenly and they lay in a heap on the ground.

"Jesus, Frances, not again," his jaw dropped open.

"What are we going to do Johnny?"

He paused for a moment and looked into the distance. Then he turned and looked directly at me.

"Don't worry Frances, I'll look after you," he promised as he took me in his arms.

"I won't leave you. I'll stand by you," he hesitated, "and the baby."

*chapter six*

NOT LONG AFTER that we were walking along Henry Street, looking in the shop windows and chatting. I stopped outside a boutique and admired a blouse. I wanted to go in and have a look at it and Johnny came with me. I looked around the shop for a few minutes and then suddenly I noticed that he'd disappeared.

I thought nothing of it presuming he was bored with the women's clothes and must be waiting for me outside, but when I came out a few minutes later I discovered he had gone.

"Maybe he met a friend," I thought. "I'm sure he'll back sooner or later."

I walked down to Mary Street and stopped to talk to a girl I used to know at school who now worked on a jewellery stall. She used to give me discounts on the earrings and I liked talking to her, she knew all the gossip in the neighbourhood.

I was passing the time of day with her when suddenly I felt a tap on my shoulder and turned to see Johnny's younger brother Brian looking startled.

"There you are Frances. Johnny's over the bridge and he's looking for you."

He was out of breath from running. "He told me to come get you; you'd better hurry."

"Sure what's the rush?" I said. "Is he alright?"

"He wants you now," said Brian with a sense of urgency in his voice. "Come on Frances, he gave me £20 to come and get you."

Brian produced a crisp £20 note from his pocket as he spoke. I stared at the money and knew something was wrong—very wrong. £20 was a lot back then.

"Right so, I'm coming," I said.

I ran down the street after Brian and reached the Ha'penny Bridge. Johnny was standing at the other side looking agitated.

"Johnny what's wrong?"

I was out of breath by the time I reached the pavement on the other side. It had started to spit rain and the wind was blowing my hair into my face. He said nothing at first. That was Johnny's style; he was always cool as a cucumber. Then he reached into his coat pocket and produced a wad of cash. There were tenners and twenties and even a few fifty-pound notes in his hand. I nearly had a heart attack on the spot.

It was more money than I'd ever seen in my life and I was shocked.

"Jesus Christ Johnny, where in God's name did you get that money from?"

I looked around to see if anyone else had seen him produce the money but nobody had noticed. There were only busy shoppers on the bridge that day, rushing by with their shopping bags in hand. Johnny looked at me, his eyes twinkling with mischief and pride.

"Will you marry me Frances?" he said.

I later learnt he had performed his first robbery. Whilst I'd been looking at clothes in the boutique on Henry Street, he'd ducked into a small office in the shop and when no one was looking, he'd raided the safe.

As I stood on the bridge with the rain pelting down on me I didn't care where the money had come from. I was 15-years-old and Johnny Smith wanted me to be his bride. That was all that mattered. The tears welled up in my eyes. I reached up and put my arms around his neck. He lifted me off the ground and swung me around in the rain. I was dizzy by the time he put me down—dizzy with happiness.

"Right so," he said, proud as punch. "Let's go and buy a ring."

We walked down the street arm in arm until we came to a jewellers shop on Golden Lane. I pressed my nose against the window and marvelled at the size of the rings. There were rings with every stone you could imagine—topaz, rubies, emeralds and of course diamonds. Some were elaborate and no doubt expensive. I wondered what kind of women would wear them. Perhaps wealthy ladies who drank afternoon tea in the Shelbourne?

I giggled as I imagined myself picking up a teacup with one of those rings on my finger.

"So what do you think?" Johnny interrupted my daydream.

"How about that one at the back?" He pointed to a platinum band with three small diamonds. It was gorgeous. But it had a price tag of £175. I nearly fainted on the spot.

"But Johnny you can't possibly afford it," I was wide-eyed with shock. He smiled and took me by the arm.

"Come on, let's go and try it on."

I couldn't show the ring to my mother. I knew she would make me take it back. What's more she would have been furious. I couldn't even tell her I was engaged. Actually I told no one but my sister, Helen.

"Let's see the ring," she demanded, as we stood in the bedroom at home later on. I pulled out an old suitcase from under the bed where I kept everything Johnny gave me.

"You're to promise not to tell Ma," I said as I produced a small, navy-blue box. I opened the lid slowly and watched Helen's look of shock and admiration.

"Jesus Frances, that's a ring and a half. You can't keep that. I'm telling Ma."

"Oh please don't Helen," I cried out. "She'll beat the living daylights out of me, you know she will."

I knew my mother would make me give it back. But it was too late. Helen was already halfway down the stairs and screaming for my mother who promptly arrived into the bedroom demanding to know what she was talking about.

"I don't know what she's on about," I blatantly lied. "I'm not engaged."

My mother knew well I was lying. She whacked me over the head with her hand and the slap made my head spin.

"You show me that ring Frances," she shouted. I started to cry. I had to produce the ring. She took one look at it and said, "Right, I'll take care of that for you. You're far too young to be engaged."

Then she slapped me across the face and walked out of the room.

The next evening Johnny called to the house after work and took me for a ride on his bike.

"Where's the ring I got you?"

He noticed its absence immediately.

"My Ma took it," I said.

He was furious.

"That bitch," he muttered under his breath. "You'll have to get it off her."

My older sister Helen had recently become engaged too. She had been doing a line with a local lad for a couple of years. He was an apprentice and his wages weren't great. They couldn't afford a ring. I think that was why she told my mother. She was envious of me because she had no ring herself.

Ma kept the ring for a few weeks and in the meantime I came up with a plan. I managed to persuade her to give it back to me on condition that I give it to Helen. Of course I had no intention of letting my sister wear it.

My mother eventually gave in and as soon as I had it in my possession again I kept it. Johnny was pleased and my mother didn't seem to care. Perhaps at that stage she had resigned herself to the fact that I was going to marry Johnny Smith come hell or high water. I think she secretly thought of it as a good thing; I'd be off her hands for once and for all.

*chapter seven*

I WAS FOUR months pregnant when I got married. There was a little bump showing but I was so slight that it wasn't noticeable. Back then being pregnant out of wedlock was something to be ashamed of and nobody except my immediate family and Johnny knew about it.

I was 16-years-old at the time but I looked about 12. I was very petite in height and very slight. Even Johnny looked younger than his 19 years. We went to two different churches before we found a priest who would agree to marry us. They just didn't believe that I was old enough.

Eventually a local priest agreed to marry us. He had known me since I was a child and could vouch for my age. But I was disappointed. Our local church was not where I had envisaged our wedding. But then I wasn't thinking straight about getting married at all. In the weeks leading up to it I walked around in a daydream, imagining our perfect life together. I saw Johnny and I sharing a little house with a garden, somewhere far away from my mother. We'd have the perfect life together and I'd want for nothing.

What was I thinking? My younger sisters used to slag me, "Would you look at our Frances, she thinks she's all grown-up getting married to Johnny Smith, Ooh Johnny!" they'd sing at me as I walked down the street.

It seems unbelievable that I was so impractical but I never thought about where we'd live, how we'd pay the bills or even who would do the housework. I really believed Johnny would sort everything out. Already I'd become totally dependent on him.

The day before the wedding Johnny's older brother decided he wasn't going to be best man because they'd had a row. It didn't surprise me. Johnny was always having arguments with his family. Most of the time one wasn't speaking to the other. I found it strange, the concept of a family who wouldn't talk to each other was so different to mine. We'd scream and shout at each other but there were no prolonged silences.

Johnny used to explain it by saying that his mother was mad and I believed him.

"My auld one," he'd say, "She's as mad as a hatter. I can't stand the bitch, and she wrecks my head."

It never dawned on me that maybe he was the mad one. Back then I didn't question anything he told me. I trusted him implicitly.

The night before the wedding there was an air of tension in my home. I had gone to bed early but I couldn't sleep with the excitement. I was in the room alone. The other girls were downstairs watching television with my mother. I heard a tap on the door.

"Can I come in Frances?"

It was my father. He had a worried look on his face as he sat down beside me on the bed.

"I want to talk to you sweetheart," he said, and I knew by the tone of his voice that something was wrong.

"What's the matter Da?" I sat up in bed and looked into his eyes. I didn't like to see him unhappy. He took my hand in his; his eyes were fixed on the floor. Then he lifted his head.

"Don't do it Frances; don't marry that man," he blurted out.

"What Da? What do you mean?"

It was most unusual for my father to come out with such a statement. He was the kind of man who rarely gave his opinion and never interfered with family affairs, he left that to my mother. Besides he had never in all the four years I'd known Johnny Smith said anything bad about him or mentioned that he didn't want me to see him. I was shocked.

What's more I was hurt. These were the two people I loved more than anything in the world and I wanted them to like each other. I wanted my father to give me his blessing.

I pulled my hand away from his. I could feel the tears begin to well up in my eyes.

"I've been thinking Frances," he fumbled. "It's all wrong. He's not the man for you. I know it Frances, I know it in my heart."

I couldn't control the tears now. They came rolling down my face and I pushed them away with my hands.

"But . . . but I love him Da," I sobbed. "And you never, you never told me you didn't like him. It's Johnny Da, what do you mean he's not right for me?"

My poor father, it killed him to see me upset, what's more I knew there was no malice in his advice. He simply wanted the best for me. He sat on that bed for over an hour pleading with me not to marry Johnny. He told me I was too young, too innocent, I didn't know what I was doing.

"I'll look after you Frances," he said. "I'll help you raise the baby."

But it was too late and I was too headstrong. I was determined to marry Johnny no matter what he said. We were going to raise a family together—a happy family where no one ever fought. I was going to be Mrs. Smith.

We married on a cold, windy morning. I didn't have a wedding dress. My father couldn't afford one and anyway we didn't want to draw attention to the wedding because I was pregnant. Instead I wore a suit—a grey pinstriped jacket in flannel material with a matching pencil skirt, and flat grey shoes. I had my hair tied up in a bun and I felt very grown up. I looked like a child dressed up as an adult, but then I suppose that's what I was.

I didn't even have a wedding ring because all the money Johnny had stolen was spent at that stage. He didn't drink or smoke. He never touched drugs or gambled either. All the money went on clothes and shoes for himself. He bought a new leather coat that cost £300. It swished about his legs when he walked and I thought he looked even more handsome than usual.

We had to borrow his mother's wedding ring for the day; she never knew Johnny took it. Johnny found the ring in her jewellery box and gave it to me.

The plan was that I'd wear it until we could afford my own and then he'd return it to the jewellery box, hopefully without her noticing its absence. I didn't mind too much. I trusted Johnny to buy me a ring eventually.

Little did I realise that it would be years before he bought me one of my own and I would eventually pawn it to feed my children.

The only people to attend the wedding were my parents and his brothers and sisters. Johnny's mother didn't come because they didn't speak to each other.

But a couple of his mates came along. Johnny was the sort of guy who always had other blokes trailing around after him. The mates stood at the back of the church and sniggered throughout the ceremony. Every now and then he looked over his shoulder and flashed them a smile as if to say, "Look at me, look what I'm doing."

The wedding was a terrible let down. No one was in good form that day. My father didn't want me to marry Johnny and Johnny's side of the family was sad because his father was not there.

There was no confetti outside the door of the church; no flowers and no horse-drawn carriage waiting to carry us away. We simply went back to our respective homes having arranged to meet up later.

I felt deflated after the ceremony. I remember coming in the door of our flat and sitting at the kitchen table in my suit. I kicked off the grey shoes that were beginning to pinch my toes.

"I'll put the kettle on love," said my father, guessing how I felt.

Later that afternoon my parents and I went to the local pub for celebratory drinks. One of Johnny's sisters, two of his brothers and a few of his mates turned up for the occasion, which to be honest was a fairly sombre affair.

There was no reception and no meal. I didn't drink either, so we sat around watching the others toast our future together. Somebody ordered me a snowball, which was a non-alcoholic cocktail. I'd never had one before and I was delighted. It had a red cherry on a cocktail stick and I thought it looked too pretty to drink.

"Here's to the young couple," somebody said and everyone raised their glass. Johnny stood beside me with his glass of coke in his hand. He put his arm around my shoulder and squeezed it.

"You're mine now," he whispered in my ear.

We spent our wedding night in his father's flat—an old corporation flat around the corner from the pub. As we walked home we stopped at the local chipper and Johnny bought me a single of chips and a battered sausage.

"Here you go Mrs. Smith," he grinned, handing me the bag of chips.

*chapter eight*

WE MOVED INTO a corporation flat not far from where I was raised once we were married. It wasn't where I'd imagined us living; but at least it was ours.

Things weren't too bad at first. Johnny would go off to work on his motorbike each morning and I'd stay at home and tidy the pokey little flat. There was no question of me getting a job. Johnny wouldn't have liked it and besides I was pregnant and quite happy not to work. We got by with the little money he earned as a courier.

His older sister had given us £200 as a wedding present to get us started. It was a lot of money and we were delighted. We bought a brand new suite of furniture. It was brown and made of tweed material. I thought it was gorgeous.

His other sister gave us a fridge, a kitchen table and four chairs. There was an old wardrobe in the flat when we arrived and we bought a new washing line that his brother helped to put up in the backyard. It wasn't a bad start to a marriage.

The day we moved in I scrubbed the house from top to bottom. I got down on my knees and scoured the filthy old bath; I cleaned the toilet and all the skirting boards. I worked all day until I had welts on my hands. There were no curtains on the windows and no wallpaper on the walls, it was cold and grey, but it didn't matter to me. It was our home and I was Johnny Smith's wife.

He was lovely to me back then—kind and considerate, understanding when I got tired or sick from being pregnant. Looking back, those few short weeks when we first married are the only time in our entire marriage when I was completely happy.

We'd been in the flat for five months when the baby was born. All through the pregnancy I had no one to give me advice. I was terrified of my mother and was never able to ask her advice. I didn't discuss personal issues with my sisters. I wouldn't ask my friends and I certainly wasn't going to discuss my pregnancy with my husband. I attended the local doctor for regular check-ups but I was too embarrassed to ask questions.

The baby was born by emergency caesarean section so I was unconscious at the time. It's just as well as I would probably have died of a heart attack. I didn't know what was happening to me and nobody explained. When I arrived at the hospital I was put on an operating table. I remember the doctor saying, "We're going to induce labour now Frances."

"Labour?" I thought to myself. "What is he on about?"

I honestly had never heard the term. That's how naïve I was.

I'll never forget the first time they put little Gillian into my arms. She was so tiny and vulnerable that I was terrified of dropping her. I was so overwhelmed with joy and pride that I didn't notice anything wrong with her. The doctor told me afterwards that she had various deformities.

In fact I had no idea what was wrong with her and I needed the nurses to explain her condition to me. She had to be fed through a tube. Although I wasn't allowed to take her home I was permitted to come in and feed her in the hospital. I watched how the nurses did it and learnt how to do it myself. I badly wanted to take her home but the doctors wouldn't let me.

I loved that child so much; it breaks my heart just to think about her. I really couldn't admit to myself just how sick she was. I think somewhere in the back of my mind, I thought I could make her better.

For three months I visited Gillian everyday in hospital. Sometimes Johnny would take me on the back of the bike but often I'd go on my own on the bus.

Johnny never stayed long in the hospital with me. It was as if he couldn't handle the fact that she was sick. What's more we never talked about it. I was afraid to bring it up in conversation in case I upset him. I felt some how that it was my fault she'd been born that way. Besides I found it too hard to talk about myself.

There was a knock on the door one Sunday afternoon. I was washing the dishes in the kitchen and Johnny was out on the bike somewhere. A young guard stood in front of me. He was only a young fella about the same age as myself, he was good looking— he had blonde hair and blue eyes, but he had a cold, calculating expression.

"Can I speak to Mr. Smith?" he said, as I opened the door.

"He's not here," I said. "I don't know where he is."

"Tell him to get in touch with the Garda station as soon as he gets back," said the guard. "It's about his daughter," he added, as he turned on his heel and walked off.

I closed the door. There was something terribly wrong with Gillian. I grabbed my bag and ran around the corner to the main street to find a taxi. It was Sunday afternoon and the streets were quiet, there were no taxis in sight. I panicked; I was out of breath and in a terrible state. I was standing outside a pub and it was closed.

Then I remembered it was Holy hour and the taxi men were probably inside having a drink. I banged loudly on the door.

"Let me in," I screamed at the top of my voice. My heart was thumping. I knew I had get to the hospital as quickly as I could. I banged on the door repeatedly but there was no answer.

Then suddenly the door opened and a tall man came out. He looked puzzled and slightly annoyed.

"Are there any taxi men in there?" I screamed hysterically.

"Well, I'll have to see love. Hold on a second."

He left me standing outside while he went to see.

Just then a tall man with black hair appeared. "You need a taxi? I'm parked over here."

I got into his car, which was parked on the side of the road and I sat in the back crying.

"Get me to Our Lady's Hospital as quickly as you can," I said to the taxi man.

"What's wrong with you love?" he asked gently.

"There's something wrong with my baby," I cried.

The man stopped the car in the middle of the street and looked at me in the mirror. Then he turned his head to face me.

"There's something wrong with your baby? Jesus, you're only a baby yourself," he said.

By the time we reached the hospital Gillian was dead. I couldn't take it in. I remember looking at her little body lying on an operating table. She had nothing but a paper gown on and for some reason it occurred to me that her arms were cold. I wasn't thinking straight and my mothering instinct was still as strong as ever. I wanted to protect her from the cold, protect her from harm, I wanted her to be alive and for a while I almost convinced myself that she was.

My mother and my sister Helen arrived at the hospital later on. But there was no sign of Johnny until later that evening. When he did arrive he was gruff and non-communicative. His way of dealing with the death was to retreat into himself. I, on the other hand, couldn't hold back the tears. They came in torrents and try as I might I just couldn't stop crying.

The doctor wanted to do a post-mortem but I refused. I couldn't bare the thought of her little body being cut up. When they took her to the morgue I thought my heart would break in two.

"Come on Frances, I'll take you home," said Helen as she put her arm around me. My mother was as cold and distant as ever. She offered no sympathy or support.

A few days later Gillian was buried. We drove from the church in the hospital with the little coffin in the back of a car.

Johnny's brother had bought a plot because we couldn't afford one. It cost £150.

There was a white sheet placed over the coffin and inside little Gillian was dressed in a christening gown.

I was overwhelmed with emotion and clearly not thinking straight. All that I could think of still was how cold she must be. Before the ceremony I sent Johnny home to get a little, white cardigan for her. I can still see that cardigan; I had knitted it myself—it was tiny with small pearl buttons.

Johnny and I, my parents, my sister Helen and a few of his brothers and sisters all attended the funeral. Afterwards we piled back into my brother's car. Anto looked at me through the car window.

"What do you want to do now Frances?" he asked. He could see I was overcome with emotion.

"Just drive Anto," I sobbed uncontrollably. "Just drive."

Anto, Johnny and I drove for hours that day. Where we went to I couldn't tell you. It's all just a blur. We sat in silence in the car, driving around Dublin and every child I passed on the street broke my heart a little bit more.

I'll never forget the way my mother treated me on the day of the funeral. She had never been much of a mother to me but I needed her more than I ever did that day. We were standing in the graveyard after the funeral when she turned and looked me in the eye.

"Frances I have to go now. I've got a function to attend tonight. The girls from the hairdressers are going out for a few drinks."

She didn't even hug me or try to console me in anyway. I was in a state of shock. I couldn't take her lack of emotion on top of everything. I couldn't even speak to the woman. I stared at her in disbelief and her face was stony cold. There wasn't a hint of feeling in it. Then she turned and walked away leaving me a sobbing mess.

I didn't speak to my mother for over 20 years after that and to this day I can never forgive her for the way she treated me.

Even after all I've been through since, it still kills me even to think about little Gillian. She was my first-born and I loved her more than life itself. I can honestly say that I've never been the same since she died. Something deep inside me broke the day she died.

*chapter nine*

SHORTLY AFTER GILLIAN died, my parents split up. It had been coming for a long time. I honestly don't know how my father put up with my mother. Ironically it was she who left him. He was an honourable man who would never have left his wife.

At that stage my mother had started to work. We all wondered why. As a family we never had much money but my father's wages provided the basics. Besides, Sorcha, Patricia and Fiona were all still young and they very much needed her around. Sorcha was 15, Patricia was 13 and little Fiona was just six-years-old.

When my mother started working there was nobody there for them after school each day and no evening meal prepared. I felt sorry for them and often fed them in my flat.

This went on for a few months before Ma decided to leave. She didn't tell any of us at the time, but we later found out she'd been having an affair with a married man. She's still with him to this day. He eventually left his wife and children and moved in with her, but for years they didn't live together.

Even to think about it now sickens me to the core. She left a lovely, hard-working man and three children under the age of 15, to have an affair with a married man. What kind of woman does that? Since I've become a mother myself I've come to despise her actions even more. She didn't even try to explain what happened between her and my father.

Despite the fact that my parent's relationship had gone from bad to worse over the years my father was bereft when she left. I think he felt he had in some way failed. I felt very sorry for him so I took him into my flat with the three girls and looked after them all for a few weeks.

We were still living in the corporation flat, which had only one bedroom. At one stage there was Johnny and I, my father and the three girls living there. My brother Anto had moved out of the family home and got his own place but he often stayed with me for short spells too. There was only one double bed, which I shared with the girls, all the men had to sleep in chairs. Looking back I don't know how we all fitted.

After a while my father went to court to get custody of the three children. I was supposed to give evidence against my mother but in the end I didn't have to as it was settled outside of court. I would have had no problem standing before a judge and telling him exactly how my mother had treated them. She was never a responsible woman and there were many occasions when her three youngest children went hungry.

My father on the other hand was a hard-working, responsible individual who would have died for his kids. When he did return to our family home he found it empty. The vindictive woman had taken everything—furniture, sheets, curtains, even the light bulbs had disappeared. The poor man. Not only did he lose his wife, he had to start from scratch and buy all the household items he had acquired over the years on a modest salary. I don't think he ever fully recovered. From that day on he looked even sadder than before.

# PART TWO

*chapter ten*

LOOKING BACK, I realise the first time I tried to commit suicide was actually a cry for help. I didn't want to die but I knew I couldn't go on living as I had been. It honestly seemed like the only option open to me.

It happened after that terrible beating—the one when I'd just been released from hospital after an operation on my bowels. I'd been so sick before that at one stage I thought I was dying. My family thought so too and even the doctors in the hospital weren't sure if I was going to pull through.

After the operation however they seemed hopeful that I could recover. They told me I had to rest.

"Rest," I laughed to myself at the time.

How little they knew about my life. Rest was the least of my priorities. I was only home three days before he beat the living daylights out of me—beat me to a pulp and left me lying on the hall floor.

It was after I returned from the doctor, after I had told her about Johnny that I tried to do it for the first time—I tried to kill myself. I remember arriving back in the house that night. Aoife was with me but she was exhausted, the poor child, she went to bed early.

Johnny Smith was in bed snoring his heart out; no doubt he was tired after a long day of drinking, robbing and beating me up.

I made myself a cup of tea before bed and then I wearily climbed the stairs. As I walked into the bathroom, I was dreading the thought of getting into bed beside him. It was all I'd been thinking about since I arrived home and suddenly I realised I couldn't face doing it. I felt like running but there was nowhere to run to.

"I'll never get away from him," I thought to myself. "This will go on until the day he dies and I have no doubt that I'll die first."

He often used to say he'd take me with him if he died. I can hear his voice in my head even now.

"Frances," he'd taunt me. "You think you're going to leave me, do you? You're going nowhere. If I go, I'm taking you with me. I'll shoot you dead before I die myself. I'll cut you up into little pieces. I'll make you die slowly and painfully, I will."

I turned to look at my tear-stained face in the mirror. I didn't recognise the sad, beaten person staring back at me. I had two black eyes and a cut that was turning septic on my left cheek. My chin was bruised and the rest of my face looked raw and red from being slapped.

Then my eyes fell on a packet of painkillers on the ledge under the bathroom mirror and suddenly a thought occurred to me and it was a wonderful, freeing thought—I was going to commit suicide. I clearly wasn't thinking straight at the time. For years I had stayed with Johnny Smith because of the children but now I no longer even cared about them. I just wanted to get away; get away from this life of hell.

I grabbed the pills and searched the cabinet for another packet. Eventually I found more with some anti-depressants the doctor had given me months ago. I looked at the back of the box and found they were out of date.

"Sure what the hell," I thought. "I'm going to die anyway."

I felt like laughing, then crying, then laughing again. I was hysterical and there was a sense of urgency about my actions now. It was almost as if I had to carry out the act before the notion left me.

I poured all the pills on to the ledge in the bathroom. There were pink ones and white ones and some, which were half-brown and half-white. They looked like sweets.

"This is it," I thought to myself. "I'm going to die. I'm going to eat all the feckin' sweets and I'm going to die."

I looked at myself in the mirror and made a sign of the cross.

"God will understand," I thought. "He knows what I've been through."

Then I grabbed as many of the pills as I could and began stuffing them into my mouth. I swallowed a gulp of water and grabbed more pills. I felt them slide easily down my throat and lie on my stomach. I stood there, staring at my reflection for what seemed like a long time. The last thing I remember is feeling dizzy and sick.

## *chapter eleven*

I WOKE UP feeling dazed and wondering where I was. It took a few minutes to realise I was in a hospital ward. I forced myself to think, and slowly but surely the memories came back and with them the realisation that my suicide attempt had failed. My vision was blurred.

I knew there was a figure at the end of the bed but I couldn't make out their features at first.

When I did, my heart skipped a beat. Johnny Smith was standing in front of me with a bunch of red roses in his arms. They were as red as the pool of blood I'd lain in the night before, when he'd beaten the living daylights out of me.

"Hello chicken," he smiled sadistically and his cold blue eyes twinkled. "Did you miss me?"

"Did you miss me?" he repeated. It was like a bad dream. I had to blink for a second to check that I wasn't in the middle of a nightmare.

"Maybe I'll wake up and find that he's gone," I thought. I blinked. But no, Johnny was there alright. What's more he'd been drinking. I could tell by the expression on his face. He must have stopped off at the early house on his way to the hospital.

"I came to check up on you," he said. "I knew you'd be telling the doctors you fell down the stairs. Terrible accident that was," he shook his head in mock disgust.

"Terrible. I've been awful worried about you, awful worried. Sure I even bought you a bunch of flowers, look—red roses. I knew that you'd like them."

If I hadn't been in so much pain I would surely have laughed. Here was the man who had caused me to attempt suicide the night before, standing in front of me, looking for praise. The crazy thing was he actually believed he deserved it.

I started to hyperventilate. I wanted to speak but the words wouldn't come out. My whole body was shaking with fear. The memory of the beating he had given me was still fresh in my mind and my whole instinct was to run. Only I couldn't. I couldn't move from this hospital bed. I couldn't even lift my head for God's sake. The pain was excruciating.

Just then the door creaked open and a nurse walked in.

"Ahh would you look?" she said, smiling. "I wish someone would bring me flowers."

I watched Johnny's face. Like that he had become a different person. His expression changed from one of power and evil to that of a kind and considerate husband.

It always galled me the way he could always do that. When he wanted to he could charm the birds from the trees. Oh, he could be very persuasive, could my husband. I'd seen it a million times before and I knew all his little tricks. He smiled sweetly at the nurse and put the roses on the bed.

"I'm her husband," he said, in his best accent. He's great at putting on posh accents. You'd think he went to some boarding school on the south side of Dublin. The nurse was completely taken in.

She turned her head to look at me.

"What's wrong Mrs. Smith?"

She ran to the side of the bed and checked my pulse. It was racing. I managed to lift my head off the pillow and point in his direction. The nurse could see I was trying to speak. She put her ear down to my head.

"It's him," I pointed in his direction.

"Yes, it's your husband Mr. Smith," she said nodding her head and not understanding what I was trying to say. She looked worried.

"He's come to visit and look he's brought you flowers."

"You don't understand," I whispered in her ear. But my voice had started to go and she couldn't understand a word I said.

"What was that Mrs. Smith?"

I started to choke. It was all I could do to get the words out. I almost gave up and then suddenly a wave of anger washed over me, anger for all he'd put me through, anger for the years of pain and torture and humiliation. And with it, I had a new found power. I was going to tell the world the truth about Johnny Smith. I didn't care if he killed me. I looked him in the eye and for the first time ever he saw me defiant.

"He did this to me," I pointed at him and almost spat out the words. Then my head fell back against the pillow.

The nurse looked into my eyes and they said it all. She knew then what I was saying.

"It was him?" she said, pointing at my husband. And in the flick of an eye-lid Johnny's expression changed. Gone was the loving husband; in his stead was the real man—cruel, belligerent and scarily aggressive.

"Get out of this room, now," said the nurse with disgust written all over her face. "What kind of a beast are you to do this to your wife? Do you hear me? Get out."

The poor woman. She didn't know who she was dealing with. Johnny wouldn't take orders from anyone, least of all from a woman.

"You fuckin' whore," he snarled at the nurse. "Don't you tell me what to do, you stupid bitch. This is my wife and I'll stay here if I want to."

He was like a Rottweiler dog, foaming at the mouth and I could see the nurse was frightened.

"Right. I'm calling security," she said, as she passed him and made for the door.

Two security men arrived immediately but even they couldn't get rid of him. He was on a roll—screaming abuse and pushing them away. Until that is, one of them threatened to call the guards.

If there was one thing that frightened Johnny Smith it was the mention of the guards. He once spent a week in prison and since then he's been terrified of being arrested. Two big security men and one nurse didn't frighten him but the thought of going to prison did.

Before you could say, "boo" he was out that door. It swung on its hinges and the red roses lay scattered on the floor.

*chapter twelve*

THE FIRST TIME Johnny ever lifted his hand to me was actually the week before we married. I put it down to him being upset.

I remember walking along the street with him. It was the evening time and there were a few children playing ring-a-ring-a-rosy on the pavement. The kids were laughing and shouting to each other. Their cries rang around the neighbourhood.

The lingering smell of brewing hops filled the air from the Guinness factory, which was close by on James' Street.

Some people hate that smell but I've always loved it. It reminds me of being young and free to run around the streets.

Johnny was in a strange mood that night.

"Are you alright?" I said, looking up at him and trying to lighten the atmosphere. I wanted him to talk to me and tell me about his problems.

"Tell me what's wrong Johnny, then I can help you," I thought to myself, but still there was silence.

He said nothing. He just continued walking a few steps ahead of me with his head bent and his eyes firmly fixed on the pavement. I stopped in the middle of the street.

"Johnny, will you talk to me for God's sake?"

Suddenly he turned on me with a face like thunder. There was hatred in his eyes. It was an expression I'd never seen before. Then out of the blue, for no reason whatsoever, he hit me. He pulled back his arm and aimed at my face. The impact of the blow sent me flying backwards and I landed on the ground.

I was more shocked than anything. This was my boyfriend, my lover, and my best friend in the whole world. This was the person I ran to to protect me from my mother. My head was reeling and the tears came fast and furious.

I tried to speak but the words just wouldn't come out. It was as if somebody had stolen my voice. He had punched me in the lip and the blood was trickling onto the pavement. My whole face throbbed and my back and my neck felt sore.

I lifted my head up slowly and there he was leaning over me.

"Are you alright, Frances?" he searched my face to see what damage he'd done and then he took a tissue from his pocket and gently began to mop the cut. He looked guilty.

"Oh Frances, I'm so sorry. Will you forgive me Frances?"

He was all talk now.

"I don't know how that happened Frances. I'm just upset that's all. I'm so sorry love. You know I love you darlin' and I'd never do anything to hurt you?"

He was like a different person now—loving and kind and terribly sorry. This was the real Johnny, the one I was going to marry in a week's time. It was almost worth the blow just to have him back again.

Of course I forgave him. I knew he didn't mean to do it. He was upset, God love him and I believed it would never happen again.

"Everyone makes mistakes," I thought. "I forgive him and I love him. I will marry him next week. I will."

I didn't tell my mother. I knew she'd hit the roof and never allow us to marry.

"What in the name of all that's holy happened to you?" she said, when she saw my face.

"I fell Ma," I lied through my teeth. "I tripped over a brick and fell flat on my face."

Little did I know that this was the first of many lies I would have to tell in the coming years.

She pulled my face towards her and examined the cut.

"You fell did you?" she said. She showed no sympathy. There was silence for a minute and I prayed she wouldn't question me more. "Right so, go upstairs and put some Dettol on it."

That was it. She didn't ask any more questions but looking back I'd say she knew well I hadn't fallen. I honestly believe she didn't care if Johnny had beaten me up. She knew I was getting married the following week and she wanted me off her hands for once and for all.

"One less child to feed, one less responsibility to carry," I could imagine her thinking. My father never questioned me. My mother had told him I fell over and I think he believed her.

We married the following week and the scar was still fresh on my lip.

*chapter thirteen*

JOHNNY DIDN'T HIT me for a long time after that and we were so happy when we first married that I put it out of my head and refused to think about it.

Looking back it's hard to pinpoint when exactly a change in him occurred but it started around the time that Gillian died. He didn't drink before that. He didn't have the money or the interest.

When Gillian passed away however he began running with a different crowd. I didn't like any of them. They were rough, aggressive men; many were criminals and most were older than him. They were all heavy drinkers who spent most of their days in the local pub. I didn't tell him what I thought of them however. I wouldn't dare to tell Johnny whom he should associate with.

He started drinking with his mates; mind you he'd only have the odd pint of Harp after work. He'd never have more than one or two at a time and he didn't touch spirits.

I didn't worry about him drinking then, I was caught up in the day-to-day living. After the first baby died I soon became pregnant again. I was over the moon and took extra care with my pregnancy. I couldn't bear to lose another child.

In the meantime Johnny gave up his job as a courier and got a new job as a taxi driver. His brother lent him his plate for a few months to get him started. The idea was that he'd earn enough money after a few months to buy his own taxi. I was delighted. Taxi men earned good money at the time and with it I imagined we'd build a sound future together. We'd fill the house with kids, I thought and they'd have toys and clothes, all the things I never had as a child.

For a while things ran smoothly. He'd go out to work during the day and come back each evening. In the mornings I'd clean the house. Then in the afternoon I'd go out shopping for groceries or maybe visit my sister Helen who had recently had a baby.

Even back then I had no friends, for years before we married Johnny had discouraged me from being friendly with other girls and any friendships I'd had before I met him had long ago ended. I never thought much about it until years later. To me Johnny was always enough. He was such a dominant personality that he took all my energy and indeed much of my time. Besides, I was close to my sisters and in many respects they were my friends. They were the only people who could understand what it had been like to grow up with my mother and that created a bond between us.

After Ma left our family home, I'd call in on my father once a week to make sure he was alright. Most of the time he looked tired and worn. The house was often cold and I worried that he didn't eat properly. I'd make dinner for him and tidy up a bit. I was close to my three younger sisters and I worried about them too and in particular Fiona the youngest. They all needed a mother but she was only six when my mother left so I felt I had to watch out for her more than the others.

My brother Anto used to call around and keep me company. I was always fond of my big brother. He had a lovely, gentle nature just like my father but he wasn't street-wise. He was always getting fired from jobs and seemed to spend most of his life on the dole, but then the whole neighbourhood was on the dole at the time. You'd see the world and his wife at the unemployment exchange on dole day. It was like one big social affair.

The days passed and my stomach was getting bigger and bigger. Johnny was supportive at first. He'd sometimes tell me to sit down and relax while he made me a cup of tea. But I'd noticed a change in his personality since he got the taxi. He wasn't as loving as he used to be and he'd become more irritable too. I tried to brush it under the carpet and pretend it wasn't happening. "Just a passing phase," I thought to myself.

Then he started working nights and I saw a complete change in him. He'd come home after working through the night and having been to the early house afterwards. He was drinking more heavily now and often the money he'd earned that night would be spent.

I'd have to beg him for money to buy a few groceries. He'd give it to me grudgingly and I'd always feel bad.

"What do you do with that money?" he'd say, "Sure I only gave you ten quid two days ago."

"He's right," I'd think. "I should be more careful about how I spend it."

But as it was I could only afford the basics and we lived on chips and burgers half the time. I didn't buy clothes for myself and we rarely went out together.

The odd time I'd go to the local pub on a Sunday with Johnny and my father. Anto might join us too or Helen and her husband Alan. I still didn't drink and I always felt uncomfortable in bars. Johnny would be agitated, looking around the bar and knocking back the pints. I couldn't relax, I always felt like I was waiting for something to happen and I'd be glad to get home when the night was over.

I didn't like the affect of drink on Johnny. He was always a quiet person, he had a presence alright, but it was a silent, almost mysterious air about him. With drink on him he was a different man. He was loud and brash. He'd be over generous too, buying rounds in the bar with money we couldn't spare. I'd have to sit there and bite my lip when he did that. I knew he wouldn't stand for me telling him what to do. There was no point in trying.

"But how are we going to pay the electricity bill?" I'd think.

One night we came back from the pub. He'd spent all his earnings on beer and I was furious. For weeks I'd been asking him for money to buy a pram for the baby that was due in a matter of weeks, but he'd refused me every time, told me we couldn't afford it and implied that I was spoilt and demanding.

In just one night however I'd seen him blow the cost of a pram and more in the pub. In a fit of drunken generosity he'd bought a round of drinks for everyone in the bar. I could have cried when he did that. To make matters worse however he started a fight with one of the local punters. The man looked at him crooked and Johnny turned on him. He was only an auld fella from the area and he meant no harm. Johnny gave him a black eye and we were all thrown out of the bar.

I'd said nothing at the time but I was mortified. I'd never seen that vicious side to him. I was shocked. I managed to hold my tongue until we got home, then

I let loose. I didn't mean to but the words just flew out of mouth and I couldn't stop them.

"Why the fuck did you that Johnny?" I screamed at him as he fell into a chair in the sitting room. "That poor man, what's he ever done to you?"

He looked at me from his slumped position in the armchair. His eyes weren't focussing properly and he had a strange expression on his face, it was one I'd never seen before. I felt instinctively frightened. I knew something was coming but I wasn't sure what it was.

And then I felt it—the full force of his knuckle against my left eye. The pain went into my eyeball and straight to the back of my head. I reeled for a second, half with the pain and half in shock. Then I covered my eye with my two hands and managed to lift my head. He looked angry and guilty all at once. He stood there staring at me for a minute as if he was shocked by what he'd done. Then he turned on his heel and walked out the door, slamming it as he left.

I sat down on an armchair and nursed my eye with my hand. Then the tears started. I sat there crying until I was sure he was asleep. I could hear him snoring from the hallway so I got a blanket from the hot press and made myself comfortable on the couch in the sitting room.

I was cold, tired and my eye ached but I couldn't face sleeping with him. I lay there shivering and waiting for the morning.

*chapter fourteen*

THERE WAS NO apology the next day, not even a hint of remorse. It was as if nothing had happened between us. Johnny simply got up and made himself a cup of tea. He rarely ate breakfast and lately I'd noticed he was eating less and less.

I lay awake in the sitting room, waiting for him to leave the house. I was hurt and upset. I didn't know how to react to him. I only had a few weeks before the baby was due and I felt uncomfortable and vulnerable. I got up and cleaned the cut around my eye. The disinfectant made it sting.

I looked into the bathroom mirror and there was a whopper of a bruise, which had turned purple during the night. Then I made an ice pack with some ice from the freezer and a tea cloth. I held it against my eye until it gave me a headache. Then I put on some make-up. I lashed on the foundation—the orange one that Helen had given me, which I never wore. It covered it a little but not enough, the massive bruise was still visible and my eye looked swollen and sore. I decided to stay at home that day.

"I'll tell nobody," I thought.

The truth was I felt incredibly ashamed. I didn't want people to know. What's more my confidence was very low and I wasn't in the mood for trying to explain the incident to anyone. Anyway, who would I tell?

Helen had her own problems and I didn't want to worry my father. I knew he wouldn't be able for it. Anto was like my father and hated confrontation. There was no one to run to.

I spent the day in front of the television, but I wasn't really watching it. In my mind I was going over and over what had happened the night before. At first I felt angry and then I started to wonder if I'd done something to deserve a black eye.

"Perhaps Johnny was right?" I thought. "Maybe I am a spendthrift?"

After all he was rarely wrong about anything and I honestly believed he was a good judge of character.

"Perhaps I embarrassed him by giving out about the money? After all, he'd earned it."

My mind went round and round in circles trying to explain his thinking to myself. I wasn't thinking straight. I was making allowances for him.

And why? Because I loved him. I loved him more than I loved myself.

"Maybe this is what is meant by sacrifices in a marriage," I thought. And then I thought of my own father and how he had made so many allowances for my mother. He never lost his temper with her, no matter how nasty she was to him or to us. He held his head high and made light of it.

"If he can do it, so can I," I thought. I took a deep breath and waited for Johnny's return. He arrived home early that day, about five o'clock in the evening. I had his tea ready for him. I'd made his favourite— chicken and chips with peas. I heard his car pull up outside and the sound of the key in the door. There was a loud banging as if he was carrying something into the house and then kitchen door swung open.

"How are you chicken? Look what I have for you!" He stood in the doorway beaming as if nothing had happened the night before. I raised my head from the paper I was pretending to read. In front of him was a brand new pram.

Nothing was said about the incident the night before, and for the sake of peace I let it go. I was delighted with the pram. I knew it was his way of trying to make it up to me. I convinced myself that I'd provoked him and of course that it would never happen again.

He treated me very well in the following days. He went easy on the drink and came home early for about a week. He was kind too, loving and concerned about my pregnancy. I was so happy to have him back to normal that I forgot about my black eye and by the time the baby was born it had disappeared.

After Gillian's death I was overjoyed to have a healthy baby. I'll never forget the first time I held her in my arms. She was so tiny and she looked like a little doll.

Johnny came to see me in hospital. He seemed pleased that the baby was healthy.

"Do you think she has my eyes?" he asked, as he peered into the cot where she lay beside me. She did have his eyes too.

"Yeah, maybe she does," I said.

"She's awful pretty isn't she?" he puffed out his chest and I could tell he was proud.

There were plenty of moments like that between us. Moments when, for an instant, I thought he was the best husband in the world. I wished it could be like that all the time but now, more and more, there were days when he was in a bad mood and didn't want to talk to me; days when I found myself actually scared of him.

I did my best to ignore him when he was like that. I'd act like nothing was wrong. I'd pussyfoot around him, making sure that his tea was ready on time, polishing his shoes for him, ironing his clothes. I tried to avoid asking him for money if at all possible. I didn't want a row.

At one stage my brother Anto came to stay with us for a few weeks. He was in between flats at the time and needed a place to crash. He slept on a chair in the sitting room at night, as there was no room for him in the bedroom. One day Anto arrived home with a motorbike.

"Look at what I found, Frances," he said proudly, as he wheeled the big bike through the hall door and straight into the sitting room.

"Jesus, Anto would you ever leave it outside? I've just cleaned these floors," I said to him.

"I can't, Frances. It would be nicked if I left it out the front and anyway it needs a bit of cleaning," he paused.

"You wouldn't do it for me, would you Frances? I've got to meet one of the lads about a job. Go on Frances. I'd be ever so grateful," he grinned knowing well that I wouldn't refuse him.

I agreed to clean the bike while he went off for the afternoon. Before he left he made me promise not to let Johnny near it.

"But why Anto?" I protested knowing well there would be nothing I could do to stop Johnny if he wanted to give the bike a spin. He was mad about motorbikes and this one was far more powerful than the little one he had himself.

"Just don't Frances," said Anto as he left.

I spent the afternoon cleaning the bike until it shone. I've no interest in motorbikes but I have to admit I was quite proud of my handiwork. It looked brand new by the time I'd finished—it gleamed. Funnily enough it never occurred to me that the bike could be stolen. The thought just didn't enter my mind.

I'd just finished with the bike when Johnny arrived home. He took one look at it and fell in love. It was a lovely big motorbike with a high-powered engine and he was like a child who wanted to play with a new toy.

"It's Anto's," I warned him. "He'll hit the roof Johnny and besides I've spent all afternoon cleaning it."

"Go on Frances. Just a short spin and then I'll be back. I'll just take it around the corner."

There was nothing I could do to stop him. Off he went on the back of the bike grinning from ear to ear.

"Where's the bike?" Anto demanded when he got home.

"Johnny took it for a ride," I said. "I'm sorry Anto. I tried to stop him but he wouldn't listen to me."

My brother nearly had a heart attack on the spot.

"Jesus, Frances," he looked worried. "That bike is stolen. If the cops see it, we'll be in big trouble. I haven't even changed the registration plate."

Johnny didn't return for hours. Anto and myself sat in the kitchen and drank tea.

"Do you think he's alright Anto?" I was worried he'd been arrested.

Just then there was a knock on the front door. It sounded urgent.

"Jesus it's the guards Anto," I jumped out of my seat and ran to the door where I looked through the keyhole to check.

It was Johnny, out of breath and flustered.

"Here, help me get this in the door, quick as you can now. The cops are after chasing me the length and breadth of the city; the bastards. That fuckin' bike is stolen."

We fell about the place laughing that day. Mind you, that was the first time I'd ever known Anto to steal anything. He wasn't the criminal type; he was too soft. He didn't stay long with us that time. Johnny and himself had a fight one night in my father's local pub.

I'd been there with my father, Helen, her husband Alan and Anto. We were having a quiet drink on a Sunday evening when Johnny stormed into the place. He was in a bad mood from the start and he began putting me down in front of everyone. It had become a habit with him at that stage and I don't think he knew he was doing it, but others noticed and of course my family didn't like it.

"Would you ever lay off Frances," said Anto to him all of a sudden. "You're always fuckin' slaggin' her about something."

That was it. Johnny lost the rag.

He pulled his arm back and in the space of a few seconds he'd punched poor Anto in the jaw. There was blood dripping off his chin. Anto looked stunned for a second then he punched him back; he got him on the cheekbone. In no time at all the two of them were brawling like schoolboys on the bar floor. My father and Helen's husband tried to stop them but it was no good. Both were thrown back on to the floor and they eventually backed off.

It took the big, burly barman to separate Anto and Johnny and then he threw us all out of the pub. But the fight continued on the footpath outside. At one stage they ended up in the middle of the street and only stopped when a car came to a halt, having narrowly missed killing them.

Both Johnny and Anto were in a bad way afterwards. They parted eventually, screaming abuse at each other. I was terribly upset. I loved them both and I hated to see them fighting. Anto had to get 12 stitches in his head and he never forgave Johnny. He stopped coming to stay at our house and shortly afterwards he got into drugs in a big way. For a while he used to sell them to feed his habit.

Heroin was rife in Dublin at the time and particularly in the inner city. Nobody in the area had a job or any hope of finding one and many of them got hooked on drugs. The lucky ones who managed to get the fare together got out and made their way to America or England. Most of them never returned.

Sadly my lovely brother was one of the victims of that drug which took people's souls and ate into the flesh on their faces. Before he tried heroin, he used to smoke the odd joint. He was never much of a drinker; he liked the smoke much better. I used to give out to him, warn him to stay away from it, but of course he wouldn't listen to his younger sister.

"Sure it's no harm, Frances," he'd say. "It helps me to relax".

It sounds clichéd but like many others he started on hash and in no time at all he was playing with the big boys and hooked on heroin. First he started smoking it and then injecting. I hated to see him using drugs. We'd been warned against them as children and I'd seen so many of our neighbours go down that road. I spent hours pleading with him to stay off them, but it was no good.

Over night he became moody and distant. He was like a different person, not the brother I'd looked up to as a child; the one who had been there for me when something went wrong.

Around the same time he started on the drugs, he began to dabble in petty crime. He'd steal the odd car and sometimes he'd lift a handbag or a wallet. I worried now that he'd get caught but he was a grown man and there was nothing I could do to stop him. Then Johnny started on the same game.

Not drugs mind you, he's always been far too wise to go near any sort of drug, but he did start stealing on a regular basis.

A few months after he'd been given the taxi plate, his brother decided to take it back. I didn't blame him. Johnny hadn't saved a penny. All the money he'd earned was going on drink and his brother was disgusted. The whole idea had been that he'd be able to buy his own plate.

"Jesus, Johnny, how are we going to live and what about the baby? We have to feed her," I pleaded with him when he told me the news.

"Don't worry. I'll get another job," he promised.

Once he lost the taxi plate, we had no money to live off except the dole and that barely covered our rent, it didn't feed us. All his mates were criminals—petty thieves who lived off the proceeds of crime and it was they who encouraged him to steal.

I remember him coming home one night with a credit card.

"What's that you've got there?" I asked.

He was sitting at the kitchen table and playing with the card, pushing it along the formica surface of the table. He looked up, his eyes shining and grinned at me.

"It's a credit card. I robbed it from a woman in a bar. Look, it's one of those gold ones." He was like a cat that had brought home a mouse and wanted praise.

"Well at least we can eat tonight," I sighed. We'd so little money back then and anything we had he spent on alcohol. Of course I didn't like him robbing but I knew we wouldn't be able to live if it were not for the money he stole.

"Anyway," I used to tell myself. "It's only temporary. Soon he'll have a real job. We'll be a respectable family with lots of money."

I lived most of my life back then in a daydream.

*chapter fifteen*

WHEN AOIFE WAS a baby, she used to sleep at the end of our bed in a cot. It was one Johnny's sister had given me when she was born. I'd taken it home and washed it, given a lick of fresh paint and it looked like new.

I was lying in bed one night with the cot at the end. Aoife was a year old at the time and she had just started to sleep through the night. She was fast asleep and I was beginning to nod off when I woke to the sound of the front door closing. I could hear a clatter and a banging noise as if he was taking something into the hallway.

I listened to him coming up the stairs. I never knew what kind of humour he'd be in and I used to lie awake in bed, listening to hear his footstep so I could gage his mood.

If his step was heavy, it was a bad sign. It was lighter than usual tonight and he was obviously trying not to wake the baby, but I heard him fall against the wall in the hallway nonetheless. That meant he was drunk.

The door banged open as he entered the room. That set the baby off. Aoife was bawling her eyes out in no time. The noise went through my head and I jumped out of bed and ran to comfort her. I hated to hear her cry.

"Would you stop all the noise, Johnny," I pleaded with him. "Shh, the baby, you woke the baby," I repeated.

"I'm sorry," he slurred, as he fell into bed fully dressed. He was rotten drunk. I could smell the booze off him and his eyes were blood-shot, but at least he wasn't in fighting form and I heaved a sigh of relief as I lifted Aoife out of the cot and carried her into the sitting room of the flat.

Johnny was out cold on top of the bed before I got to the door, still with his coat on and his two shoes hanging out the end. It was pitch dark and as I fumbled for the light switch in the hall, I nearly fell over something.

"Jesus what was that?" I said out loud as I regained my balance with the baby in my arms. I turned on the light and there was a black refuse sack on the floor of the hall. I looked around me and there were about ten of them, all full to the brim.

Johnny was snoring loudly in the bedroom and I wasn't going to wake him to ask what they were, but I was intrigued. The baby had stopped crying at that stage and her little head was nestling on my shoulder. She seemed sleepy so I tiptoed into the bedroom and placed her in the cot. I held my breath for a minute to see if she settled. It worked; she was asleep. Then I ran back out into the hallway. I couldn't contain my curiosity.

What on earth had Johnny Smith brought home?

I pulled open one of the bags. It was like opening Christmas presents under the tree as a child.

"Jesus, Holy Mother of God," I said. Inside were the contents of what looked like a gift shop. Different types of crystal wrapped in boxes—vases and glasses and funny looking ornaments, huge bowls that sparkled. I looked at the labels: Waterford Crystal.

"Waterford fuckin' Crystal!" I said to myself. "Where on earth did he get this?"

Then I opened the other bags one by one. Some had more crystal and others were full of fur coats. They were real fur. I could tell by the quality. There were coats of all shapes and sizes and in different furs too. I guessed that some of them were mink. There was another bag full to the brim with ornaments— Wedgewood and China, expensive figurines and clocks that you'd have on your sideboard.

"Where did he get these from?" I muttered to myself. I knew well they were stolen. I tried on one of the coats. It came to my ankles and I swung around in it, holding it over my chest. It felt lovely, warm and soft.

I was getting tired at that stage so I went back to bed and slept. I dreamt I was walking through Dublin in a mink coat, the end kept trailing in the mud and it bothered me.

It was the next morning before I had a chance to confront Johnny about where the stolen loot had come from. He was very vague, skirting around the issue and refusing to give me a straightforward answer. But then that was Johnny for you. He'd rarely tell you outright where anything came from.

He was all pleased with himself mind you. He took the ornaments and pieces of crystal out of the bags one by one and placed them around the living room—on the mantelpiece, on top of the television, even on the floor with the baby crawling around in between them.

"Johnny, they're gorgeous," I had to admit I was impressed.

Then he threw one of the mink coats at me and I tried it on. "Look at me," I laughed, as I turned around pretending to be a model in the coat.

"You look like Sue Ellen from Dallas," he said and we both fell around laughing. I didn't tell him about my dream.

Later on that morning he went off to "work". Work was now robbing.

"More lucrative and less hassle than taxi driving or running around, delivering packages on a motorbike," he used to say. I didn't argue. I had a baby to feed and another one on the way and I was happy just to make ends meet. I was two months pregnant with Molly at that stage.

Later that evening there was a knock on the door. I was alone in the house with Aoife. I knew it wouldn't be Johnny, he was out working, and I rarely had visitors. I peered through the keyhole to see a tall guard outside.

"Oh my God," I thought. "I can't let him in." I knew exactly what he was looking for and the front room of the flat was covered with all the stolen merchandise Johnny had acquired.

The baby was asleep so there was silence in the house as I tiptoed into the bedroom with my heart beating like mad. I sat down on the bed and listened to the doorbell ringing for the second, the third, then the fourth time. Each ring became more insistent and my heart beat faster as they did.

"What on earth will I do?" I thought. Suddenly I started crying. I felt angry and helpless. I didn't want to be the wife of a criminal but Johnny had given me no choice in the matter.

I sat there crying and hoping the baby wouldn't wake up so the guards wouldn't find out we were there. I couldn't even ring Johnny as the phone was in the hall, they'd hear me if I rang and there were no mobile phones back then. Eventually they gave up and I heaved a sigh of relief as I watched them drive off.

When Johnny came back at dinnertime I told him what had happened.

"Okay. We've got to get rid of the stuff," he said, trying to act cool but I knew by his tone he was worried. If there's one thing that ever scares him it's the thought of going to prison.

"If we're caught, I'll be arrested for fuck's sake," he turned on me. You'd think it was my fault.

"I didn't steal them," I shouted at him. "What were you thinking of, bringing them back here?"

He stormed out of the kitchen.

"Come on," he said. "We've got to be quick. They could be back any minute."

I followed him into the sitting room, annoyed that he'd walked out of the room before the argument was over but aware none the less that we had to move the stuff quickly or we'd all be in trouble.

"But where will we put them?" I said. He paused for a moment and stared out the sitting room window.

"In the canal," he answered.

We spent ages wrapping up the crystal, the fur coats and the ornaments. Then we loaded them into black refuse sacks and I kept sketch while he reversed the car and we carried them out of the flat.

I was exhausted by the time we reached the car but thankful the guards had not returned before we got rid of them. Both of us were convinced it was only a matter of time before we got another knock on the door. We knew they wouldn't give up that easily. They must have got a tip-off from someone; perhaps it was one of the neighbours.

Johnny's face was sweating and worried as he drove off with the black bags in the boot of the car. I heaved a sigh of relief however and went back inside. I made myself a cup of tea and sat in the kitchen, listening to the clock tick. I waited for the guards to show. I waited for hours that night, sitting there thinking about what I was going to say. I've never been good at lying, it just doesn't come naturally to me and I was worried they'd see straight through me.

I needn't have worried. They didn't come back. I was still at the kitchen table hours later when Johnny arrived home. He'd dumped the refuse sacks in the canal at Portobello Bridge. Nobody saw him, he said, as he sat down in the kitchen.

"Remember, when they come back, we know nothing," he looked me in the eye, making sure I understood.

The guards didn't come the next day, or the day after that or the following day either. In fact they never came back to inquire about the stolen goods and it was only days later that we realised we'd over reacted.

All those beautiful pieces of crystal and fur coats lay in a heap at the bottom of a dirty canal. I doubt anyone ever found them and if they did the ornaments and glass would be broken and the coats ruined. Years later we laughed about it but at the time it killed us. To this day I think about that mink coat. I've never had a fur coat and there have been plenty of winters when I've been without any coat at all.

I soon got used to Johnny bringing strange things back to the flat. One time he arrived home with a load of shoes and on another occasion he had boxes of cigarettes. He would never tell me where he got the stuff, or what he did with it afterwards, but I knew it was stolen. To be honest I didn't want to know; it was easier that way.

One day he brought home a wedding ring with "I Love You" engraved on the inside. I knew he'd stolen it but I didn't care. I was over the moon. I now had my very own wedding ring to wear.

Mind you I still held on to his mother's ring although I didn't wear it. I had to find the right time to return it. After we married Johnny rarely saw his family. The odd time one of his brothers would call around but he didn't keep in touch with his mother at all. I suppose he didn't need her now, he had me.

It didn't take Johnny long to get used to robbing as a way of life. He'd go out to "work" as he called it first thing in the morning. When the kids got a bit older and started school he'd make up the fire before he went while I gave them breakfast. Then he'd drive them to school before he began his day's work.

He always dressed well. His love of expensive clothes never left him and even if we had no money for food he'd make sure to buy the best of clothes and shoes. He needed to dress well for "work" he used to say.

He had all his suits made for him by the best tailors and he'd buy his shoes in Brown Thomas, or Fitzpatricks's on Grafton Street. Nothing but the best was good enough for our Johnny. And he'd fool anyone he met. He looked like a well-to-do businessman. He could play the part too. He always had a talent for accents.

I've seen him switch from a working class Dublin accent to a Dublin 4 whine like that and then back again in a blink of an eyelid. He could pretend he was American or Scottish, or whatever the situation required and I'm sure he fooled many a tourist with tall tales before he slid his hand inside their handbag and stole the all-important credit card.

He loved stealing credit cards. I think he found it easier than lifting a handbag or carting home stolen merchandise. He never robbed houses mind you. Anything he brought home he acquired from one of his friends, or took from a shop or car.

He had no guilt about stealing. Johnny had never been religious. What's more the men he hung around

111

with all stole to make ends meet and he was easily influenced by them.

They all drank heavily and he got into the habit of stopping off at the early house for a few drinks before he began the day. All his mates would gather, they'd have a few pints or a shot of whiskey as they talked. The drink would calm their nerves from the night before—"the hair of the dog" as they say.

It never did to have the same criminals working the same areas. They'd discuss what parts of Dublin they were going to work. They'd rob from hotels and restaurants, shops and people on the street, they'd pickpocket little old women on the buses and they'd steal money from the wealthy students on Grafton Street. Many a night Johnny came home drunk out of his mind and boasting about how he'd robbed from a famous pop star or a politician. The more well-known the person was the better, and of course the bigger amount of money he'd stolen the more he'd boast.

*chapter sixteen*

YOUNG FRANCES WAS born three years after Molly and she too was perfectly healthy. I now had three lovely girls and I was extremely proud of them all. Aoife was four when Frances was born.

At that stage Aoife and Molly were old enough to share our double bed and young Frances slept in the cot. Fiona my sister would also sleep in the double bed if she stayed over and she often did. In many ways I took the place of her mother. None of us kept in touch with Ma; she had her own life now and she didn't seem to care about us.

I don't know how we all fitted into the one-bedroom flat. Luckily we were able to move to a new house just after young Frances's birth. Johnny had put our names on a council housing list when we married and we were offered a two-bedroom semi-detached house in a sprawling estate outside the city. My sister Helen lived five minutes away so I was delighted.

"This will be a chance to start again," I thought to myself. "It'll be a new beginning. Maybe Johnny will ease up on the booze and get himself a real job."

I moved into the new house full of hope. We didn't have many belongings to take with us—just a few pieces of furniture that we loaded into his brother's van. I remember opening the door of the new house and walking into the hallway—my hallway.

It was cold and drab, but it was a house, not a flat and it even had a little garden out the back and a patch of greenery in the front. There was no wallpaper on the walls and we had no carpets, but I was determined to make the place homely and set about cleaning it immediately. I asked Johnny to buy curtains and he reluctantly agreed. I had no say in what he bought however and he arrived home drunk one evening with green and brown patterned drapes. They were horrible but at least they kept the room insulated and gave us some privacy so I didn't make a fuss. Of course he didn't pay for the curtains. They, like everything else he acquired, were bought with stolen credit cards.

He used the cards to buy everything under the sun and became an expert at fraud. He'd steal the card and use it that same day, signing with the same name as was on the card. He was great at impersonating people's signatures. Mind you, he never gave me cards to buy things myself and he'd only dole out the house keeping money under duress.

He'd often arrive home with "presents" as he called them. Although he had good taste in clothes for himself he'd bring home horrible things for me to wear. It was as if once we were married he didn't want me to look good. He was extremely possessive and he'd be furious if another man even looked at me. I think that was why he wanted me to dress like a middle-aged housewife. I was still in my early twenties then and though I say it myself, I had a good figure. I never got a chance to show it off however. My younger sisters used to slag me.

"Look at those granny clothes you're wearing Frances," they'd say and they were right. I was forced to wear long skirts and dull looking cardigans that hid my figure and made me feel anything but attractive. I never had high heels or pretty dresses and I felt embarrassed walking down the street. I knew no man would look twice at me.

The credit cards couldn't pay for our household bills, however. To this day I get a sickening feeling in my stomach when I see a bill of any sort land through the letterbox. In the past I worried constantly about how I was going to pay bills. I'd have to get him in a good mood and then ask him ever so subtly for the money. Chances are it would begin a row.

I did my best to avoid any confrontation with Johnny. I only asked for money when it was absolutely necessary, it was too much hassle and it would always end in tears. I was becoming more and more scared of my husband.

He was moody and unpredictable back then and he was drinking more than ever. I'd smell it off his breath the minute he walked in the door. Although he'd started by drinking lager he soon moved on to Guinness, and by now cider and gin and tonics were his tipples of choice.

I started having the odd glass of shandy a year or two after we married but I never got drunk. I didn't want to and anyway he wouldn't have liked it. He used to give out about other men's wives who drank too much.

"Whores," he'd call them. "Drunken Whores." He was always talking about women in a derogatory way. He really didn't like them much.

I was becoming lonelier and lonelier. I had drifted away from my family because Johnny didn't like me mixing with them. I rarely saw Anto. He'd become totally addicted to heroin by this stage. The odd time I did meet him on the street and it killed me to look at him. His face was all shrunken and he had a distant, pained look in his eyes. It was as if he wasn't really there.

Then I heard through my sister that he'd got himself a girlfriend and was moving to England. I heard about his girlfriend Cassandra before I actually met her, and when I did, I have to admit I didn't like her. She was a loud, brash young one from Dublin and she, too, was on heroin. I had always thought Anto would fall for someone gentle and sweet just like him, but thinking about it now, maybe it's only natural that he'd go for someone stern and loud. They say men choose women like their mothers.

They only knew each other a few months before they decided to move. Both were on methadone at the time and they believed they had a better chance of staying off the drugs if they left Dublin. England seemed like a good option, Anto had heard there were jobs in construction over there. I hoped he could make a life for himself and I phoned to wish him well.

"Thanks Frances," he said to me on the phone. "We're going to try. This will be a new start for us now. Frances," he paused. "You look after yourself, now."

"Of course I will Anto," I said reassuringly.

"No really Frances. I mean it."

I put down the phone and cried to myself. I found it hard to take affection from anyone. I wasn't used to it and if I let down my guard and felt sorry for myself, even for a few minutes, then I felt I would fall to pieces. I wiped away the tears and gave out to myself for crying. I put Anto out of my head and got on with the daily chores.

Life carried on and a few months later he phoned to tell me he was off the drugs and had got himself a job as a counsellor in a community centre. He was now counselling young children who had become addicted to heroin. I was pleased for him, pleased that he was picking himself up and making a life for himself.

I still saw Helen the odd time. She lived around the corner and it was hard to avoid her when we first moved in. I kept in touch with Fiona too. I tried to visit my father once a week but I could never stay long.

Johnny hated me being away from the house for any length of time. If I left I had to tell him where I was going and when I'd return. He used to phone the house about ten times a day just to check that I was there. If I wasn't in when he rang, he'd hit the roof and I'd pay for it later with an argument.

I hated fighting with him so I'd do whatever it cost to keep him happy. I'd visit my father and then rush back to the house so he wouldn't be angry with me. Looking back I realise I was totally under his thumb but at the time I didn't realise, I just wanted to keep the peace.

To give Johnny his dues, he was good with the kids while they were young. When he was in a good mood he'd play with them. I always remember him lifting them off the stairs in their pyjamas and carrying them into the sitting room so they wouldn't have to feel the cold tiles on their little feet. He'd lift Aoife first, then Molly and they'd squeal with joy.

"Look at me Ma," Aoife would shout.

When they questioned me about his job I told them he drove a taxi, that he borrowed it from his brother and gave it back each evening so they never saw it.

He'd often bring home presents for the children— toys or clothes or sweets, everything was bought on other people's credit cards, even the lollipops and bars of chocolate.

Johnny always had problems apologising. His way of getting around it was to spend. Whenever we fought he'd bring home something for me the next day. Sometimes it was a household item like an ornament or set of plates, on other days he'd have a pair of shoes or a piece of jewellery for me. I didn't want his presents, I'd have preferred an apology any day, but I'd say nothing.

The fights became more frequent and we were becoming more distant. What had started as a loving and happy relationship had by now turned sour.

He seemed to have lost all respect for himself and also for me. The truth is I was afraid of him and he knew it. That gave him a sense of power, which he just couldn't handle. He began by verbally abusing me whenever we'd fight. Then he started to hit me every now and then. At what point it became a habit I'm not sure but I do know it coincided with his drinking. The more he drank, the more aggressive and ultimately violent he became.

The violence was sporadic at first. Weeks would go by sometimes without a fight and during those times I'd try to keep the peace. Trying to keep Johnny in a good mood was like stepping on eggshells; I'd never know when he would blow up in my face. I became more and more nervous and that just seemed to annoy him. I started to believe that I was at fault.

"I'm just an irritating person," I used to think. "If I did everything he wanted then these fights wouldn't happen. Next time will be different," I used to promise myself. "Next time I'll make a special effort."

He'd cause a fight over the simplest of things. Something as simple as his dinner not being ready at six o'clock. I'd always bring it in to him in the sitting room so I could feed the kids in peace. He loved brown sauce, but if for example, I forgot to bring it in with the meal then there would be hell to pay.

He'd start jeering and taunting me. I'd say nothing at first. I'd sit on the sofa and stare at the ground. I'd try counting to ten.

"Just count and keep on counting until he stops," I'd think. "Let him think he's won."

But it didn't work. The anger would build up in me. It was a terrible overwhelming anger and Johnny always knew exactly how to provoke a response in me. He knew which buttons to press. I'd sit there listening while he ranted and raved about the fact there was no brown sauce on the tray.

I'd take it at first, breathe deeply and keep counting. I used to think that if I tried hard enough I could drown out his voice with my own in my head. It never worked. What got to me more than anything else was his tone—a high-pitched, abusive tone that tortured my mind. If it were anyone else I'd have been able to handle it, but not him.

Suddenly he'd have pushed me too far, I'd explode—let loose. The words would hop out of my mouth as if I had no hold over them. That was when the real trouble began. Then he'd smile that old sadistic grin of his.

"Think you can answer me back? Do you? Think you're better than your husband?"

"I'll answer you back if I want to," I'd scream in rage.

"How dare he," I'd think, "How dare he talk to me in that way."

But that would enrage him all the more. He'd swing his arm back and aim for me. Then I'd get it; straight in the jaw. I'd fall back with the pain and the pressure would send me flying against the sofa. And then he was off.

Once he'd thrown the first punch there was no stopping him. Next he'd go for my lip, then maybe land a black eye on me. He'd keep on punching me until I was a grovelling mess—cowering on the ground, sobbing uncontrollably.

The children would be crying in the kitchen. Little Aoife was only a toddler when the beatings started. She'd come running in and stand over me, looking at her father in shock as he went back to his dinner, staring at the television as if nothing had happened and shovelling food into his mouth like there was no tomorrow.

Then he'd get up, say nothing and walk out. I'd sit there and weep, pitiful tears of pain and anger and helplessness. I'd wait to hear the front door slam, knowing then that the coast would be clear. He'd be gone to the pub for the night and I'd have nothing to worry about until he came back drunk out of his mind, when the pub closed.

*chapter seventeen*

I DIDN'T TELL anyone about the beatings. As I said before, I wanted to block them out of my mind. What's more I felt helpless. I had to stay with my husband for the sake of the children. I had no income and no way of earning money. I'd only ever had a job for a few weeks when I was 16 and besides, my confidence was so low that I honestly believed I wasn't capable of working.

Johnny used to tell me I was stupid.

"Ignorant, ugly and fat," he used to call me. "Sure how would you ever hold down a job and what other man would have you?"

I believed him. It didn't occur to me to tell the guards either. I was brought up in a community where the police force was scorned. To inform the guards of a crime, any crime at all, was considered the lowest thing you could do. I thought of them as enemies rather than people who could protect me and anyway I thought, "What good would it do?" If they did bar him from the house I'd be on my own with the children and we'd be destitute.

I'd heard about shelters for battered wives but I knew little about them. I imagined them as horrible places where poverty-stricken women queued for soup and slept on flea-ridden mattresses with their children. There was no help-line that I knew of at the time and no media coverage of domestic abuse. It wasn't that long ago but women suffered in silence back then and so did I.

I tried to make the best of our life together. I lived for the days when he was in a good mood and I looked forward to seeing my family or little treats like cream buns in the afternoon, or watching Dallas on television. I know now that it was no life. I was young and beautiful and in my prime. I should have had a social life and friends. I had neither.

The only time I ever got to go out in the evening was when he decided to bring me out on the town the odd time. Then I had no choice; I had to do what I was told to. I never had anything pretty to wear and I'd have rather stayed at home, but he would insist that I come with him.

He'd arrive home and announce that he'd booked a meal for us in a restaurant. They were always

124

expensive restaurants too. Johnny didn't do things by half. Besides he got a kick out of spending other people's money so the more expensive the better and he'd pay for it all by credit card.

He'd make me dress up for the occasion and then we'd drive into town. Fiona usually minded the girls so we wouldn't have to worry about them.

Those times should have been good but I was always so worried about getting caught that I honestly didn't enjoy them. My heart would be in my mouth from the moment we'd walk into the place.

"Good evening Mr. ' so and so'," the waitress would say as she hung up his expensive coat. He'd call himself by the name on the credit card. We'd sit in the restaurant and I'd feel horrible. He always looked so better dressed than I did but I couldn't let him know how I felt.

"What's wrong with you?" he'd say. "Are you not having fun? Come on now, give us a smile."

I'd smile nervously and look around the room. I envied those other people. Ladies dressed to the nines in pretty dresses and high-heeled shoes, laughing animatedly with their husbands. They had no idea how helpless and scared I felt.

I'd be determined to make the best of the situation but looking back it was comical. Johnny would sit there and read the wine list.

"Give me a bottle of your most expensive wine," he'd say to the waitress in his grandest accent. He didn't even drink wine usually but he knew how to put on an act. Then he'd order the most expensive items on the menu. We regularly ate lobster, fillet steak, and caviar. Mind you our fridge at home would be empty and I wouldn't have the money to buy a loaf of bread. But in the restaurant, we'd eat ourselves silly and order dessert.

"Have anything you want," he'd say proudly. You'd think he was paying for it himself. He'd sit back in the chair when he'd eaten all he could and smile benignly at the waitresses.

You had to admire him. He knew how to play the wealthy businessman. I'd laugh to myself. "If only they knew where we came from," I'd think. "If only they knew the truth."

Johnny would drink most of the bottle of wine and then he'd ask for another one. I'd sit there and pray he wouldn't get too drunk.

He was always clever though. He knew when not to draw attention to himself. We'd finish the meal and pay for it all by credit card. Johnny would leave a generous tip. Then we'd saunter out of the place as if we were the wealthiest couple in the world. Johnny would put his arm around me as we left and the other customers would smile graciously.

The manager of the restaurant would open the door for us and we'd sail through it, nodding and smiling.

"We must come here again," my husband would say in a loud voice.

I'd smile just to keep him happy but inside I'd be a nervous wreck until we got home. I always had a feeling the guards would be after us as soon as they found out about the card.

We'd avoid going back to the same restaurant for a while in case they remembered us, but we went to all the best places in Dublin.

I remember one day Johnny rang me in the middle of the afternoon.

"Pack your bags."

I could tell he was excited by his voice. "We're going to have a night of luxury."

"Jesus, what has he got in mind now?" I thought to myself. He was always so unpredictable and although it was one of the qualities that attracted me to him in the first place, it unnerved me now. He arrived home that evening, all excited, like a little child.

"We're going to a posh hotel in town," he announced. "I've booked us in."

I hadn't planned on going out and I had no babysitter for the three children. Young Frances was still just a baby.

"But Johnny I can't possibly go to a hotel. What about the kids? I can't leave them on their own."

I knew the thought wouldn't even have occurred to him.

"Sure can't you get a babysitter?" he said, annoyed that I hadn't been pleased at his harebrained idea.

"Or your sister Helen, sure ask her?"

I hated having to unload the girls on Helen. She had enough to worry about but I knew there was no other way. It would be too late to get a babysitter and there was no way he'd take no for an answer. I got on the phone to Helen and she agreed to take them for the night.

We arrived at the Westbury Hotel in the city centre in our best clothes. Johnny had bought me a dress for the occasion—a cotton, knee-length dress with pink and black flowers. It was prettier than anything he usually brought home and I was pleased. As usual we were treated like royalty by the staff. They smiled and nodded as we walked into the hotel restaurant where we enjoyed a slap-up meal and two bottles of champagne.

"Bring some more champagne to the room waiter," Johnny slurred but he kept up the accent. We were staying in the penthouse suite that night.

The next morning he once again paid for everything with a stolen credit card. Looking back I don't how we got away with it. We'd always be careful about what name we used. It had to be the same as the one on the card. We've been in every restaurant and all the best hotels in Dublin. In later years we even went on package holidays to Spain and everything was paid for with stolen credit cards. We never once got caught.

*chapter eighteen*

I GOT BAD news one day about Anto. My sister phoned me to tell me that he was HIV positive. "HIV positive?" I said. I didn't even know exactly what it meant until Helen explained. I hadn't heard from my brother in a long time. I knew that he had a family but I'd never met them. I thought what a pity it was that they didn't know my children, their first cousins.

The girls were getting older at that stage and we never brought them anywhere. There were no trips to the zoo or the cinema, or even the park. I was too scared to do anything without Johnny's permission so sometimes I'd ask him to bring them out for the day.

"Ahh, go on Johnny," I'd say. "They're only young and they should be out seeing things like other kids their age."

One day he agreed to take them to Malahide beach. Our neighbours had two little girls around the same ages and they were going.

I knew the neighbours to say hello to. I'd stop and make small talk when Johnny was out and they'd invited us to come along. It was a lovely, sunny day and I knew the girls would be delighted but I was nervous. I found myself increasingly nervous back then. There was always the fear that Johnny would let us down, but as always I determined to make the best of the situation.

"Maybe he'll be on his best behaviour," I thought. I fooled myself into believing that things would run smoothly.

I packed a picnic. Then we all bundled into the car and followed the neighbour's car in front of us. The sun was shining and Johnny was in great form, singing songs as we drove along and getting the girls to join in. They were beside themselves with joy, jumping up and down in the back of the car.

We found a sheltered spot on the beach and spread out a rug to sit on. Our neighbours were nice people. They were a little bit older than us. Their children were well-behaved little girls; Sharon was seven, a year older than Aoife and Fiona their youngest was the same age as Molly. Young Frances was still only two-years-old. She was walking by then and I couldn't take my eyes off her.

The kids were overjoyed to be playing on a beach. They'd never seen sea or sand for that matter and they took to it like ducks to water. Aoife jumped up and down with excitement, "Oh Ma, this is so great, I love it here Ma, I want to stay forever."

The girls made sand castles and ran around in the sunshine while I unpacked the picnic and made small talk with Fidelma. She was a nice woman with a kindly face and I felt relaxed in her company. I was good at putting on a front for strangers. I'd smile and pretend I didn't have a care in the world. I'd act as if Johnny and myself were a loving couple. Inside however I'd be praying that he wouldn't give the game away, insult me in front of them or lose his temper with the kids.

No matter how much of an act I put on I always felt different to other women. Their worries seemed trivial compared to mine because I lived on the edge. It always created a void between us. The fact is I was a battered wife and they were not. I often wonder whether people like our neighbours knew the truth about Johnny. Did they guess what he was like? Perhaps they'd heard the rumours, people must have gossiped about us. Looking back I realise they probably thought me standoffish, or cold and unfriendly.

That day on the beach Johnny was on his best behaviour. I couldn't believe how charming he was and I was delighted.

"Maybe this is the new Johnny," I thought. "Perhaps the bad times are over." He was all charm, pretending to be a loving husband, a great father. The neighbours lapped it up and I sat there grinning watching young Frances totter around on the sand.

Things ran all too smoothly for about an hour and a half. I should have known it was too good to be true. Suddenly Johnny stood up and looked at his watch.

"I just remembered Frances, I have to meet someone," he said, as he looked down at me from his standing position. The sun was directly behind at him and it blinded me when I looked up at him.

I was taken aback. I knew well he hadn't made an arrangement to see anyone. He was going to the pub. I could have killed him. Here he was letting me down in front of our neighbours. I didn't know what to say.

"I won't be long," he added and I could hear the guilt in his voice. He checked his watch again. "It's half two now. I'll be back in an hour."

There was nothing I could say so I smiled sweetly, "Do you really have to go Johnny? The kids will miss you."

But it was no good, the thirst was on him and he was determined to appease the God of alcohol. He turned and walked off down the beach to the car park. Aoife ran after him, "Da, Da come back," she shouted.

"Where are you going Da?" I could see him lift her off the ground in the distance and say something to pacify her. Then he put her down and continued walking along the sand until his figure disappeared in the distance.

I prayed he'd come back soon. I felt mortified. My neighbours sensed my embarrassment. I saw them exchange glances and I wanted the ground to open up and swallow me. Aoife came running over, "Ma, Da says he'll be back soon. He's going to buy us ice cream."

She was all smiles now, God bless her. But he didn't return in an hour. I waited and waited. The sun got lower in the sky and the children became tired and irritable. Young Frances started to cry.

By five o'clock there was still no sign of Johnny. I had no way of contacting him.

"He must have forgotten the time," I said nervously. My friends smiled sympathetically. Joe offered to take us home and then return for his own family. We couldn't all fit in his car.

"It's not a big deal, Frances," he reassured me when I objected. "Honestly I don't mind."

I agreed because I had no choice in the matter. I was stranded on a beach with three young children and there was nothing I could do.

I made my apologies. Jesus, I seemed to spend my whole life apologising for my husband's behaviour and then Joe drove us home. The journey took an hour and a half and young Frances cried for most of it. Poor Joe had to turn around and drive all the way back again to collect his own family.

The children were glad to go to bed that night. Exhausted by their day on the beach they fell asleep instantly. I, on the other hand, tossed and turned. Eventually I nodded off about eleven o'clock, only to be woken an hour later by Johnny, drunk out of his mind as he staggered into the bedroom. He'd been drinking since he left us that afternoon.

There was no point in making a fuss. I said nothing and turned over in the bed, praying that he wouldn't want sex that night. I was lucky. He was snoring loudly beside me in no time and eventually I nodded off to sleep wondering if he'd ever change.

It was moments like that that killed me. All the time I wished for a normal life. I didn't want much—a regular marriage and a husband I could depend on. I didn't desire a big house and lots of money. I wanted my children to grow up happy and in a safe and comfortable environment. I wanted them to have the childhood I never had.

I suppose I lived half of my life in my head, refusing to face reality. I really convinced myself that this was just a passing phase. Johnny and I had been so in love when we first met and deep down I still loved him. Every time he let me down, every time he hurt me and upset and angered me, I forgave him. I believed marriage was for life and the thought of leaving him just didn't occur to me. Besides, where would I have gone and who would have supported us?

Every now and then I begged him to give up the drink.

"Please Johnny, stop drinking," I'd say. "If not for me, then do it for the sake of the children."

But it was no good. He'd often cut back for a few days, maybe a week at a time, but in no time at all he'd stagger home. He was clearly hooked. Although I had yet to admit it, even to myself, Johnny was a full-blown alcoholic and he was in a state of denial.

*chapter nineteen*

FIONA, MY YOUNGER sister, was affected by his drinking too. She had been staying with me on and off for years. We were closer than sisters, and I've always had a special relationship with Fiona; she too took after my father.

One night Johnny made me go to the pub with him and we left Fiona babysitting the girls. She was 15 years of age at the time. I didn't know but Fiona had just begun to smoke.

In our absence she climbed out the sitting room window to have a cigarette. She knew the smell would linger if she smoked in the house and she didn't want to wake the girls upstairs by opening the front door. After the cigarette she climbed back in immediately but one of the neighbours across the road saw her getting back through the window. It was raining and she had a duffle coat on with the hood up at the time. They thought she was a burglar and called the guards.

I'll never forget arriving home to a guard car sitting in the driveway. Inside the guards were interrogating my poor sister. They checked the whole house and found nobody there of course, but Fiona was too terrified to tell the truth. She knew that Johnny would beat her up if he knew she'd been smoking so she pretended she hadn't climbed out the window at all.

"I don't know what you're talking about," she kept on repeating to the baffled guard.

"Just tell the truth Fiona," Johnny piped up pretending to be a caring brother-in-law.

"It's alright," I nodded reassuringly. "We won't be angry if you tell us the truth love."

She broke down and told them what had happened. When the guards left, Johnny turned on her. The poor girl was terrified. He screamed at her for two hours solid. He didn't hit her mind you but his tongue was worse than his fist. He could kill you with it; leave you a grovelling mess with no will to live.

Fiona never liked to see Johnny in a bad mood with me, it upset her.

"Why do you take it from him, Frances?" she used to say after he'd verbally abused me, tore me to shreds with his tongue. Fiona was a teenager at that stage and she was full of all the spirit that comes with youth.

"Sure what can I do Fiona?" I'd say to her and there would be despair in my voice. I was increasingly despairing back then. I felt trapped and helpless.

I had no friends to confide in and even Helen and myself had drifted apart. Johnny had become increasingly paranoid about me talking to other people. If I left the house for any length of time he'd time me and there'd be hell to pay if I didn't make it back within the allotted time. I rarely went to the shops because he didn't like it. I'd ask one of the girls or Fiona to run around to the local newsagents whenever we ran out of bread or milk.

I remember one afternoon when Helen called around unexpectedly. I was doing the dishes in the kitchen and he was lazing around the sitting room watching the football on television. Aoife ran into the kitchen.

"Ma, aunty Helen is coming up the road to see you," she tugged at my apron and looked up at me. I panicked. I knew Johnny was in a contrary mood and there'd be trouble if I brought Helen into the house, besides he'd already started drinking for the day and I knew he'd cause a scene, I'd be mortified in front of Helen who didn't know the full extent of the situation.

I thought quickly.

"Tell her not to come in," I said to Aoife, as I pulled off the rubber gloves I'd been wearing to wash the dishes. I tugged off my apron and threw it on a chair.

Then I checked my appearance in the mirror we had hanging over the kitchen counter. I looked worn out and sad but there was no time to put on any make-up. I ran to the front door and looked out. I could see her coming up the road with a plastic bag in her hand.

"What are you doing?" he'd heard me opening the front door.

"Oh nothing, I'm just checking on the kids," I shouted back nervously, hoping he wouldn't come out to the hall.

Helen got as far as the front gate, which was locked. I ran out to see her and stood at the gate.

"Ahh, Helen," I said, trying to act relaxed. "How are you doing? I haven't seen you in a while."

She smiled.

"You never call around anymore Frances," she said and I could see she wasn't pleased. "You shouldn't be a stranger."

I paused for a second. How was I going to get out of this one? I knew Helen would smell a rat.

"Can I come in?" she said, automatically opening the gate.

"Look I've brought us some nice biscuits. Come on, make me a cup of tea and I'll tell you all the gossip. Did you hear Matilda Walsh is pregnant?"

Matilda was one of our neighbours growing up. I'd have loved to hear about her pregnancy and all the gossip. I hadn't seen Helen for months and I was dying to sit down and have a chat with my sister, but I couldn't. I knew he'd kill me if I brought her in.

"I'm really sorry Helen, but you can't come in," I said looking at her apologetically. My poor sister, she thought I was being cold and unfriendly towards her.

"What do you mean I can't come in?" she was understandably shocked but I didn't care what she thought. All I thought of was keeping Johnny happy, making sure there was peace. If I had to offend my sister, then so be it. I knew I could make it up to her again.

"No Helen, thanks for coming over but you can't come in today. Johnny's doing a few things around the house, fixing a table in the sitting room at the moment, he's very handy these days."

I pretended to laugh. I amazed myself sometimes; I'd become such a good liar.

Helen was taken aback.

"Well okay, Frances, if it's not a good time I understand," she said but I could tell by the tone of her voice that she didn't understand. She understood nothing because I hadn't told her about Johnny. I wanted to tell her but I couldn't. If I told Helen it would weaken my position even more. What's more I was ashamed to admit the truth to my sister.

She stared at me for few moments, searching my face with her eyes for the truth. She knew me well and this was out of character. Eventually she said goodbye.

"Are you alright Frances?" she asked before leaving.

"Ahh sure I'm grand Helen. Bad timing. That's all," I held her eye for a second and I wondered afterwards if she knew something was up. She handed me the bag with the biscuits before she left.

"You might as well have them," her voice was sad and hurt.

I turned and walked into the house feeling lonelier than ever.

"Who was that?" my husband shouted from the sitting room over the noise of the football.

"Nobody Johnny," I shouted back, trying to make my voice sound upbeat. "Just a young fella, selling scratch cards."

I think Helen took it personally that day because we lost contact for a long time after that.


Johnny's paranoia was hard for the children too. He didn't want them to have friends. He wouldn't allow them go further than the garden gate to play during the day. They had to stay in the back garden, the front garden or else inside. I'd let them out for a little while when he was gone to work but if I thought he was on his way home I'd be out like a shot and chasing them back in again.

"Quick, your Da is on his way home," I'd warn them. They were good children and they'd come running back into the house but they didn't understand.

"Why can't we play with the other kids, Ma?" Molly asked me one day. I didn't know what to tell her. I had no answers.

Aoife and Molly became close because they weren't allowed to play with the other children. I don't know what the neighbours believed. They must have thought we had notions of ourselves. The irony is that outside the house, Johnny appeared to be the perfect father. He got up early and drove them to school everyday. He'd collect them in the afternoon and drive them home again. All the teachers thought he was great. They'd smile when they saw him coming.

The girls had all the best clothes too. He'd buy everything on credit cards so they wanted for nothing. They were the best-dressed children on the road but they had no friends.

On another occasion Johnny announced he was taking us to Butlins. We'd been married for nearly ten years by then but we'd never once been on a holiday. The children were ecstatic when they heard. They talked about it non-stop for days on end. You'd think we were going to Disneyland.

Johnny had been on the dry for a few days before we left and I was ever hopeful. We packed our bags up for a week at Butlins and bundled into the car. Everything ran smoothly for the first two days. Johnny didn't touch a drop of alcohol and it was like being with a different person. He was kind, caring, and considerate and the children were in heaven. They played on the amusements and went swimming in the pool. I'd sit and watch them during the day and look at all the other happy families, couples who cared about each other, who were respectful and openly loving. How I wished I had that kind of relationship with my husband. It made me melancholy to think about it.

We were there two days when things started to go badly wrong. The children were exhausted and hungry on the second evening and we took them back to the chalet where we were staying to get them changed before dinner.

I was struggling to get young Frances into a dress when Johnny announced he was going to buy chips.

"Could you not wait for your dinner?" I looked up at him from the bed where I was sitting dressing Frances; she was irritable and crying now.

"I want ice cream, Ma," she kept whinging. I think it was beginning to annoy him. I begged her to stop but she wouldn't.

"I won't be long," Johnny shook his head. "I'm starving, sure I'll be back in half an hour."

I let him go. I didn't really have a choice in the matter and anyway I wanted to keep him in a good mood. Johnny could be lovely when things were going right and he wasn't drinking.

"Okay then, I'll wait here with the kids for you," I said as he closed the door behind him. He didn't come back. I waited and waited and after two hours there was no sign of him. The children were hungry and so was I. What's more they were bored, they wanted to get out of the tiny chalet and play. I had painted my nails and changed into a dress while he was gone, now I sat there on the edge of the bed, counting the minutes.

"This is ridiculous," I thought. "Where in God's name could he be?" Suddenly I'd had enough. "You stay here and look after your sisters," I said to Aoife.

"Lock the door behind me and don't let anyone in unless it's your Da," I cautioned her. I stormed out of the chalet. I hated leaving the children on their own but I had no choice. I had to find that man and give him a piece of my mind.

It wasn't difficult. All my fears were confirmed as I entered the bar. Not only was he drinking however, he was sitting there chatting up two young blondes. I was furious. He'd left his wife and three hungry children for two and half hours while he sat drinking with two young ones wearing mini skirts. He turned to look at me as I came in.

"There you are, I've been looking for you," he said. The girls giggled mischievously and I felt mortified. I was ashamed to have this man as my husband. I stood there for a moment, feeling confused. I was torn between letting loose and telling him exactly how I felt or saying nothing in front of the women. They were about the same age as me but I felt dowdy, unattractive and very ashamed beside them.

I stared at him for a moment, searching for words that wouldn't come. Then I turned on my heel and left. I marched back to the chalet and began packing our clothes. The kids were relieved that I'd returned.

"Are we going to dinner now, Ma?" said Aoife. The poor things were starving, they hadn't eaten since lunchtime.

"No darlin', we're going home," I announced. I wasn't sure how we were going to get home at that hour of night but I knew that there was no way I could stay there. The one thing I had never thought Johnny capable of was being unfaithful. In all the time I'd known him he had never so much as looked at another woman in my company. He actually used to give out about other men who would cheat on their wives. Every now and then he'd go on a sanctimonious rant when he he'd had a few drinks to loosen his tongue but still not enough to fall over. Now I'd caught him red-handed chatting up two dolly birds at the bar. I was shocked and disgusted, on top of everything else he'd put me through this was too much.

Suddenly there was a bang at the door, then he barged into the room. There was guilt written all over his face and I could smell the drink.

"What are you doing Frances?" he demanded to know as I packed up our belongings. "We're going home, Da," piped up Aoife. "Ma says we have to go but I want to stay Da, can we stay Da, please?"

He turned to me.

"I was only talking to them Frances, can I not have a quiet drink and make a bit of small talk for God's sake? Why do you always have to go and overreact?"

There he was as usual, turning things around, making them my fault and not his, and implying that I was the one with the problem. He was so good at it too. He never failed to make me question myself.

"We're going home, Johnny," I stood my ground. He looked at me for a moment and then his expression changed. He was angry now and not repentant anymore.

"Right so," he motioned to the kids. "Come on, into the car."

We drove in silence for two and half hours. The children fell asleep quickly, even Aoife was exhausted and they could sense their father was in a bad mood. It was 10 o'clock at night by the time we reached the house and I was glad to get home. Once more I felt despairing and foolish.

"I should have known better than to agree to a holiday in the first place," I thought.

He was furious. We were only home half an hour before he turned and began abusing me.

"Paranoid," he called me. "Paranoid and possessive."

I didn't trust him, he said. "And what was a relationship without trust?"

Looking back I have to laugh. If I don't I'll cry. Somehow he made me believe that he was right. He opened a can of beer as he shouted at me and I went to bed with a black eye and bruises all over my chest that night.

## *chapter twenty*

IT SOUNDS STRANGE to someone who has never experienced it, but I got used to being a battered wife. As the years went on, Johnny drank more and the violence increased. I can honestly say that I lost my confidence entirely during that period, but it was a gradual loss. Life was one long roller coaster ride and in a perverse way I was hooked. I hated that ride with a passion but I'd bought the ticket and I couldn't get off.

There would be days, even weeks sometimes, when Johnny was in great form. He'd be kind and loving and all that a husband should be. But as the years progressed those times became fewer and fewer, and after a while they ceased to happen at all.

All of us were the victims of his terrible temper and abuse of alcohol. I worried about the girls, all three of them lived in as much fear of Johnny as I did, and the older they got the more it showed. They began to ask me questions.

"Ma, why can't I bring home my school friends like other girls can?" said Aoife to me one day. I didn't know what to say. How could I explain that her father was an alcoholic, control-freak who wanted nobody to get close to them.

Because Aoife was the oldest, she witnessed more of his abuse than the other girls. I could see her becoming introverted and shy, as she grew older. She was always a sensitive child and I don't think she was able to see her mother beaten up on a regular basis.

Molly, of course, was affected too but she seemed to have more spirit; she was always the one to answer him back when none of us dared to. Aoife too would sometimes tackle him, then he'd hit her too.

The abuse didn't stop at me; he'd now started beating his own daughters. I remember one time when he hit poor Molly over the head with a saucepan. It was a Sunday afternoon and Molly who was only 10 at the time, had been helping me make the dinner in the kitchen. When the meal was ready, we all sat down together to eat it. Johnny pulled the table up close to him and I put his dinner down in front of him.

I hadn't even sat down myself when he turned on Molly.

"What the fuck are you looking at?" he roared at the poor child.

"Nothing Da," she said in all innocence.

Like that Johnny was on his feet, he pushed the table away from him and his dinner fell on the floor. Gravy trickled down the leg of the table. Then he grabbed a big, heavy saucepan from the counter and threw it at Molly. It landed on her head. I can't imagine what it felt like. Molly can barely remember but she fainted immediately. The poor child was lying on the floor unconscious with blood dripping off her head.

"Jesus, Johnny you've probably killed her," I screamed as I ran to her side. Her face was white as a sheet and I called an ambulance immediately. By the time she regained consciousness Johnny had vanished. He didn't even wait to see if she was alive.

It took weeks for the wound on Molly's head to heal. Luckily she wasn't seriously injured but to this day she has a huge scar on her scalp.

Living in fear does strange things to your body. The two older girls and myself suffered with bowel problems for years. It became a regular occurrence for us to rush to the toilet whenever Johnny rang to announce he was on his way home. There would be queue outside the door and we'd all have diarrhoea from sheer terror.

He always rang beforehand, as I said he was phone-happy. He'd ring constantly throughout the day to check up on us. He'd want to know the whereabouts of all the girls, what's more he'd quiz me on everything I'd done that day, whether I'd been out of the house or had met anyone. He was becoming increasingly paranoid.

If I talked to another man he would accuse of me having an affair. It makes me laugh to think about it now, simply because there was no way I was capable of having an affair at the time, even if I'd wanted to.

I was constantly worn out, depressed and I looked horrible. People actually tell me that I look younger now than I used to. My skin was pasty and lined back then. I did no exercise, I got very little fresh air and I lived on a diet of bread and chips with the odd battered sausage or burger thrown in.

Johnny still took me out the odd time for a drink. He arrived home early sometimes. "Come on," he'd say jovially as if we were the happiest couple in the world. "I'm taking you out."

I never wanted to go. More often than not I'd have a black eye that was still fresh from the last time he'd beaten me up and I'd know make-up wouldn't hide it. I'd become an expert at covering the bruises and cuts on my face. I could have been a make-up artist for God's sake.

Over the years I tried everything—toothpaste, talcum powder, tea bags, anything to heal the wounds he'd inflict on me. I wore the darkest, most orange-coloured foundation I could find. I'm naturally fair so I must have looked ridiculous, but I didn't care. I just wanted no one to notice. Of course people did notice. I became used to sympathetic glances from women and men alike. People on the street, teachers in the school, strangers on buses.

I remember once being in the bus station when Aoife was going on a school tour. A woman I had never seen before turned to me.

"Would you like a cup of tea love?" she asked me out of the blue. I blushed profusely.

"No you're alright. Thanks anyway," I replied immediately. I felt embarrassed but I wasn't sure why.

Years later, when I looked back, I realised she must have felt sorry for me. Maybe she suspected that I was being abused. At the time I just wanted to get away from her. I would never have talked about my situation to anyone, least of all a stranger.

Mind you, most of the time, no one ever questioned me. It's just as well as I wouldn't have told them the truth and it would have added to my shame. I lived my whole life in a state of abject shame—shame that destroyed my youth, crippled my personality and trapped me in a state of despair. They say that guilt is a way of controlling people and in my case it worked. I felt guilty about everything; guilty if I ate too much, guilty if I watched television, guilty if I gave out to the kids, guilty if I answered Johnny back and overwhelming guilty if he hit me.

On one occasion we were in a bar with Fiona, Helen and her husband. He actually hit me in public that time.

And he hit me often. It was like a bad habit that he couldn't resist. I suppose it gave him a sense a power, it made him feel like a man. Little Johnny Smith was master of the universe in his own home and gentle as a lamb outside it. He didn't need a reason. If one of his friends annoyed him for example he'd come home and take it out on me. Anything and everything annoyed him and I was always the one who suffered as a result.

I don't think any of our neighbours guessed what went on behind our front door. Maybe they heard the screams, but if they did, they turned a deaf ear to them. And Johnny was a different person outside the house. He used to bring home sweets for all the children on the street.

They'd run to the car when they heard him coming and he'd open the door slowly and theatrically. He loved a bit of drama.

"Mr. Smith," they squeal with delight. "What have you got for us today?"

He'd pretend to search his pockets as the children gathered around him, some on bicycles, and some just out of nappies.

"Sorry kids, I've nothing for you today," he'd joke with them.

"Ahh, go on Mr. Smith, give us a lollipop," some cheeky youngster would pipe up. "We know you have them."

Then he'd give in and produce lollipops for the entire road and chocolate bars and ten-penny bags. The kids would jump up and down with delight and run off to show their mothers. A few would be standing, smiling in their doorways.

"Isn't he a lovely man? So generous with the children," they'd nod their heads and smile in approval.

"Say thank you to Mr. Smith now, don't forget your manners."

It killed me to see the way he could fool people. I felt like running out and screaming at him in front of the neighbours, but it would have done no good. He'd have told them I was mad, and who do you think they would have believed? I was beginning to think I was mad.

All kinds of thoughts went through my head when I was alone. I'd think about murdering him in the middle of the night but I knew I'd never be able to carry it out. Sometimes I'd daydream about running away but I honestly didn't know how I'd look after the children. I believed myself incapable of earning a living, and for years Johnny drummed it into my head that I was stupid, "Stupid and neurotic, ugly and unable to talk to people."

I thought there was no hope. I carried on living but I wasn't really living, I was merely existing. I wasn't even 30-years-old and I felt like my life was over.

*chapter twenty-one*

I DREADED THE thought of sleeping with him. I used to go to bed early every night and do my best to fall asleep before he came in. Sometimes I'd cover myself up in layers of clothing. Looking back, I suppose it was a form of protection but it never worked.

"Where do you think you're going with all those clothes?" he'd sneer at me. "Do you think you're in Siberia?"

Sometimes when I'd gone to bed before him, he'd leave me alone. Besides I always felt safer in bed. I'd often get into bed with the girls. Aoife and Molly shared a double bed in the back room. I'd climb in beside them, thinking that I'd have less of a chance of being wakened by him because he'd have to waken them too. But more often than not it didn't work.

"Frances," he'd slur from the landing. "You've got two minutes to get in here or I'm going to come and get you."

I'd be too afraid to disobey him so I'd crawl out of bed sheepishly and into my own. On one occasion, he came into the room and grabbed me the hair. Then he hauled me, kicking and screaming into the next room. Of course, the kids woke up and witnessed the whole scene. That killed me more than anything. I hated for them to be upset. The two youngest started to cry and I was helpless to comfort them at the time. He was already slobbering all over me like an animal in heat.

I dreaded having sex with him. He'd climb on top of me and go at it like there was no tomorrow. His heavy body crushed me in the bed and his hands were all over me. The smell of alcohol would make me want to vomit.

He didn't care if he hurt me; in fact, he seemed to get a perverse sense of pleasure from it. Sometimes he'd pinch my nipples really hard to see how I'd react. On a number of occasions he pulled out a bunch of my pubic hairs just to make me cry with the pain, then he'd laugh sadistically.

He'd roll over and fall asleep immediately with not a loving word or an emotional embrace. I'd lie there, stare at the ceiling and listen to him snoring. I felt horrible at those moments. I felt dirty and used and violated.

Johnny had no scruples. He blatantly lied all the time and I caught him out on a number of occasions. I remember one Christmas when the two girls wanted sovereign rings as presents. The rings were all the rage at the time and all their friends had them. For weeks before I begged him to buy them.

"Don't worry, I'll have them by Christmas," was all he'd say and his tone of voice would imply I was over-reacting.

But I wasn't. I'd spent enough years with him to know that he was likely to forget all about the rings and spend the money on drink instead. I didn't want to let the girls down. I'd saved a little out of any housekeeping money he grudgingly gave me, since as far back as August and I reckoned I had enough to buy one ring, but where on earth was I going to get the money for the second one?

By Christmas Eve there was no sign of the rings, what's more there was no sign of Johnny. He'd been gone since early morning. Christmas was a great time for robbing. The streets would be full of wealthy shoppers, laden down with bags and oblivious to the pick-pocketing ability of Johnny Smith.

It was always a great excuse to drink too, not that Johnny ever needed an excuse but in the run up to it I wouldn't see him for days on end. He'd be either out stealing money and credit cards, or in the pub with his mates, boasting about how much he managed to graft that day.

I dreaded Christmas with a passion. I was always worried sick about how to buy the Christmas clothes for the children, the groceries for the dinner and there were other expenses too like a Christmas tree and presents. For weeks before I'd always be nagging Johnny to get whatever the kids wanted and I'd be sick with worry about it. Never mind the tension in the house and the violence which always happened on Christmas day. It was one big nightmare.

That year, I decided I would have to give Aoife the ring I had bought and I'd give my own sovereign ring to Molly.

The three girls came running down stairs on Christmas morning. We had a little plastic tree in the living room that Johnny had brought home one night. I think it came from a shop, it had definitely been used before but I didn't mind. I was happy that we had one at all. I remember the grins on their faces and the shrieks of delight as they searched the tree for presents. I used to wrap up their presents and hide them in the tree so they'd have to look for them amongst the branches and the fairy lights.

"Oh thanks Ma, it's fabulous," Aoife grinned, as she unwrapped her ring.

Molly ran to hug me. "Oh Ma thanks a million."

Young Frances was too young for jewellery. She got a plastic tea set, which pleased her no end.

The worst thing about Christmas day was the fact the pubs were closed. Johnny never bought me Christmas presents but he'd be sure to stock up on the beer in the house. We'd all go to mass in the morning, leaving him behind with the beer and he'd usually be locked out of his mind by the afternoon.

He'd sit in the sitting room, watching the queen's speech and giving out about everything under the sun. He used to rant when he was drunk; rant about the cost of a pint, rant about neighbours, and rant about how great he was.

The girls and I would pussyfoot around him, nodding our heads in agreement and smiling to keep the peace. Aoife and Molly were becoming almost as expert at keeping him sweet, as I was. They knew never to disagree with him and to obey his every command.

After lunch I'd get the dinner ready in the kitchen, praying that maybe this year would be different, maybe this year he'd nod off to sleep before he caused a fight. But it never happened, every Christmas I'd end up in tears and more than likely I'd have a black eye and bruises to show for it too.

Back then Johnny always made sure to aim for parts of my body that wouldn't be seen. The girls would end up crying and all of us would go to bed early. I often went at eight o'clock simply to avoid him. I'd lie there and wait for him to climb the stairs, dreading the thought of having him on top of me.

*chapter twenty-two*

WHEN MOLLY WAS 13-years-old she ran away from home. Johnny had grounded her for two months prior to that because she had answered him back. That meant she was allowed to go to school and the rest of the time she had to spend in the house, confined to her bedroom. He went mad if she even came down stairs during that time.

"Get up to your fuckin' room," he'd scream at her.

The poor child, my heart went out to her and I used to let her come down when he wasn't around but there'd be murder if he found out. She was miserable during that time and I felt helpless to alleviate her pain. She had confided in a school friend about just how badly Johnny treated her, and the two of them decided to leave after school one day.

When Johnny came to collect the girls, Aoife was waiting for him alone.

"Honest Da, I don't know where she is," said Aoife who knew nothing of her plan.

Johnny was furious by the time he came home.

"Where the fuck is that child?" he roared at me.

"I don't know where she could be Johnny, I hope she's alright," I said.

I was worried that she'd gone and done something stupid.

"I'll try calling Tanya's house."

As it happens Molly and her friend Tanya had hopped on a bus into town. They'd wandered around O' Connell Street, feeling somewhat bewildered and wondering what to do. Then Molly phoned my sister Fiona who was staying with us at the time. She told Fiona that she was going to stay in Tanya's house, of course, Fiona came straight back and told us. I think Molly knew that Johnny would be mad when he found out but he'd be more likely not to hit her if she was in someone else's house. Johnny and myself got into the car and drove to where Tanya lived.

"I'll fucking kill that young one," he said as he drove along the road. "Who does she think she is running away from home?"

I was terrified for Molly; I knew what he was capable of.

"Ahh Johnny, she's only young and she doesn't know what she'd doing," I tried to explain.

"Shut up you," he turned on me. "She wouldn't have done it if it wasn't for you encouraging her to pal with that young one Tanya."

There was nothing I could say.

Tanya's mother was waiting for us by the time we reached the house in Crumlin and the two girls stood behind her, looking guilty.

"There you are sweetheart," said Johnny to Molly in his best accent. He'd suddenly switched on the charm in front of the other woman. "We've been awful worried Molly, are you okay pet?"

He was like a different person now, all gentle and understanding. Molly glared back at him and said nothing. Then the three of us got into the car.

Poor Molly was beaten black and blue that day. I had to keep her out of school for three days and of course I got a hiding too.

Shortly after Molly ran away, I got a windfall in the form of compensation from an accident. I'd been involved in a car crash with Johnny a couple of years before and as a result I'd injured my neck. We'd stopped at traffic lights and a car had crashed into us from behind.

Johnny had persuaded me to sue, I didn't want to at the time, I was so shy back then I would have been happy to let it go, but a few years later I was delighted to receive the money. It was only a couple of thousand but it was more money than I'd ever had in my whole life.

I felt like a child at Christmas and my mind raced as I imagined all the things I could buy. "Maybe a new cooker for the kitchen or a lamp for the sitting room? Perhaps I could even buy some pretty clothes or a pair of shoes?"

Of course, Johnny had other ideas.

"Why don't you buy yourself a little car?" he suggested slyly. He had no car at the time and he wanted one for himself.

"But I can't drive Johnny," I said, shocked at his suggestion. I wasn't allowed to leave the house on foot never mind by car.

"Sure you could get yourself a few lessons and learn," he said as if it was the most obvious thing in the world and the fool that I was, I believed him.

Within a week, I'd handed the money over for a car he brought home and I'd booked myself in for driving lessons. I was excited at the prospect. For years I had never even considered learning to drive. What was the point? I knew Johnny wouldn't allow it. Now however he seemed happy to let me learn and a car would open up my world. It would give me the sense of freedom I longed for.

The driving instructor was a gentle, middle-aged man who was very patient with me. I was terribly nervous to begin with but little by little I surprised myself by picking it up. I was delighted. For once in my life I felt like I was bettering myself.

My happiness didn't last long. Johnny arrived home early one day just in time to see me get out of the instructor's car. I was grinning at the time, my driving had improved no end and the instructor was pleased. I waved to him as he drove off and I turned the key in the door.

My husband was waiting for me inside. He'd watched the whole scene from the window and he was ready to explode. He followed me into the kitchen and I could tell by his heavy step that he was angry.

"You think you're great now, don't you?" he taunted me as I nervously laid my bag on the kitchen table.

I had my back to him. I was afraid to turn around. I said nothing, hoping, praying that he'd calm down.

"Look at me," he roared. "Look at me you filthy bitch."

I turned around. I was afraid to disobey him. Then he grabbed me by the shoulders and shook the living daylights out of me.

"Tell me truth," he demanded.

"Johnny," I whimpered. "Johnny, what are you talking about?"

"Tell me the truth you dirty cow," he stared into my eyes. "You're having an affair with that man, I know you are, you might as well come clean. You're having an affair with that driving instructor."

I felt like laughing and crying at the same time, his accusation was so ridiculous.

"Johnny, don't be stupid," I said. "There's no way that's true, of course I'm not. Sure he's a married man Johnny."

But there was no winning with Johnny Smith.

"Are you calling me a liar?" he was even angrier now. "Calling me stupid, are you?"

He spat in my face. He was always spitting in my face. It was another of his degrading habits.

"I'll show you. You're my wife and I'll fucking show you."

With that he started shaking my shoulders with his two hands, then he let me go and I fell to the floor. I was crying now, crying with fear for what was to come, crying with the sheer madness of his unfounded accusations. And then he kicked me, first in the chest and the pain went through me, then he aimed for my groin and I screamed in agony and doubled over with the pain. Then he kicked me again and again. Each time the pain was horrendous and I felt like my body could take no more.

"Johnny stop it, please Johnny, please stop," I cried out but it was no good. My pitiful cries fell on deaf ears.

Suddenly young Frances ran into the room. She was 10-years-old at the time.

"Stop it Da," she screamed. "Leave her alone Da, please Da leave her alone."

Then he turned on her. He pulled back his arm as if to hit her. Of all the girls young Frances was Johnny's favourite and although he often hit her too, for some reason she always forgave him, and if he'd listen to anyone it would be her.

He stared into her eyes for a few seconds with his arm raised, ready to punch her. But he didn't. She held his gaze while I lay whimpering on the kitchen floor, curled up in the foetal position. Then he stormed out of the room.

I gave up the driving lessons after that and he took over the car. Months later he let me take them up again and this time I got a female instructor. Then he told me I was a lesbian. I gave up altogether. Johnny didn't want me to drive.

The irony is that he'd often ask me to meet him in a bar. I hated having to do it but I'd have no choice in the matter. If I refused there'd be trouble later. I remember one time he rang home in the afternoon.

"Can you meet me in the Gate on James Street? I want to talk to you."

I had to get the bus into James's Street because he had the car. I hated getting the bus on my own. I'd become more and more introverted and terrified of strangers. When I was outside the house, I felt vulnerable and scared. I asked Molly to walk me to the bus stop.

I reached the pub at nine o'clock. There was no sign of Johnny so I perched at the bar and waited. I had no money to buy myself a drink so I asked the barman for a glass of water. I felt embarrassed to be there on my own, the pub was full of men and I could see them looking me up and down from the side of my eye. I tried not to make eye contact with any of them by keeping my head bent.

A full hour passed and still Johnny had not arrived. One of the men in the bar approached me.

"Are you alright love?" he said in a kindly voice. "You've no drink there, can I get you one?"

I looked up at him and he had a nice face. I could tell by his voice he felt sorry for me but there was no way I could accept his offer. Johnny would have hit the roof and killed him when he came into the bar. I was worried too that he would walk in at any moment and see us talking.

"No really I'm fine," I said to him nervously. "But thanks for the offer."

"Go on love, have a drink. I'm buying one for myself anyway," he insisted.

"No I'm fine thanks," I began to sweat and I must have looked so worried that the man knew I wanted him to go away. He went back to his friends and I waited.

Johnny didn't arrive until 11 o'clock. By the time he got there he was drunk and we only had time for one drink before the bar closed. I was glad to get home that night. Back then, I hated being in public places and I especially hated being with Johnny whose whole life now revolved around drinking. I used to beg him to get help.

"Johnny you're an alcoholic," I'd say to him sometimes. "You need help."

But it was never any good. There was no getting through to him.

"You're the one that fucking needs help," he'd reply. "You're mad as a brush."

The terrible thing was, I was starting to believe him.

*chapter twenty-three*

ONE CHRISTMAS SHORTLY after that I got a phone call from Anto. I hadn't heard from him for a long time and I was overjoyed to hear his voice.

"Frances, are you there?" he said, and I recognised a touch of English in his accent.

"Anto, Jesus Christ, it's great to hear from you love. Are you ringing from England?"

"I'm here Frances," said Anto. "I'm in Dublin with my family for Christmas. Can I call around Frances? I know it's St. Stephen's day but we won't stay long. I'm dying to see you Fran."

Johnny had gone to the pub early that morning and because it was St. Stephen's day, I thought he'd be there all day. I was so pleased that Anto had phoned that I agreed he could come to see me, but as soon as I put the receiver I began to worry.

"Please God, please don't let Johnny come home," I prayed. "If I can just get Anto and his family in and out of the house before he comes back, everything will be fine," I thought, as I busied myself making sandwiches and tea. The girls flapped around helping me and between all of us we had turkey sandwiches and Christmas cake laid out on a tray before Anto arrived. I was looking forward to seeing my brother and his two children. I'd heard that he'd been off the drugs for a number of years now, but I knew he had AIDS. My father had told me some time ago and I wondered what affect it had had on him.

I'd read up on it and I knew there was little chance of being infected but I wondered about things like the toilet seat in the bathroom and the cup he would drink tea out of. I felt guilty but I couldn't help it. I loved my brother but my survival instinct and the urge to protect my family was stronger than any blood ties.

I nearly died when he walked into the house. He was like a walking skeleton. His features were so changed I hardly recognised his face. It was shrunken beyond belief and his eyes showed the years of suffering at the hands of an addiction.

I was shocked but I didn't want to embarrass him. He had his wife Cassandra and his two young girls with him. They were sweet, little things and I was pleased to meet them, but I could hardly hold back the tears when I looked at Anto. He was like a different person and it pained me. I suspected he not only had AIDS, he was dabbling with heroin again.

You could have cut the tension with a knife as we sipped tea in the sitting room.

"So tell me, how have you been Anto?" I said nervously as I sat down on the edge of the couch.

"Not too bad now, Frances," he smiled and then bent his head to look at the ground. He seemed nervous but pleased to see me. His wife Cassandra looked well, she had stayed off the drugs.

We talked about the kids and his life in England, he still worked at a counselling centre for drug addicts and he'd made a life for himself in the Irish community there.

Suddenly I heard the front door. My heart skipped a beat; I looked at the clock on the mantle piece. Twenty-past three in the afternoon. What on earth was Johnny doing home?

"Excuse me for a second Anto," I said, as I jumped up almost spilling the tea all over me. I ran into the hall, closing the sitting room door behind me. Johnny was standing there and I could smell the drink off him.

"Who's in the sitting room?" he slurred.

"It's my brother Anto, his wife Cassandra and two kids. They're over for Christmas, Johnny," my voice trailed off and I waited for his response. For years Johnny had hated Anto.

"That fuckin' drug addict," he used to call him. I knew the real reason he hated him was because years ago Anto had turned on him and tried to protect me.

Johnny paused for a second then he roared at me, "Get him out; get him fuckin' out of the house before I throw him out."

"Shh," I put my finger to my lip. "Please Johnny don't make a fuss. It's Christmas and I haven't seen him for years, please," I begged, trying to whisper the words so they wouldn't hear in the next room. But it was no good, there was no persuading Johnny Smith once he had a bee in his bonnet, besides he loved the feeling of power he had over me.

He grinned sadistically. "I'm going out for ten minutes, he'd better be gone by the time I get back," he turned and then looked back over his shoulder, "or you'll pay for it." He banged the door behind him.

Anto turned to me when I came back into the sitting room.

"What's wrong with you Fran?" his eyes searched mine.

"Nothing Anto, everything's fine."

Then suddenly I started to cry. I couldn't hold back the tears. It was all too much.

"Don't worry, Fran," said Anto when I told him about Johnny. "I won't let him lay a hand on you. How dare he treat you like that? You're my sister. I'll have it out with him Fran, I will." But Anto had forgotten who he was dealing with and I knew Johnny would be more than able for him.

"No Anto," I wiped away the tears. "You'd better be going, I'm sorry," I sniffled. I stood at the door waving him off and once more I felt deserted.

Johnny didn't come home until much later that evening.

"What the fuck was he doing here, that AIDS-riddled, druggy?" he shouted at me when he came in the door. I had to pretend I didn't know my brother would call.

I lost touch again with Anto for a long time after that and it's only in recent years that he's started to phone me again the odd time. I ask him how is health is and he tells me he's fine, but I know otherwise from talking to his wife Cassandra. She says he has problems sleeping. He stays up at half the night on his own and insists on leaving the lights on in the house. He's become paranoid too. He went to the dentist recently and demanded to have all his teeth pulled. He was convinced the police had installed a tracking device in his gums years ago when he was kept in prison overnight.

It makes me angry just to think about it. What kind of a dentist would have done such a thing? Cassandra said there was blood everywhere and it took him weeks to recover. Now he has dentures but he can't wear them all the time because they irritate his gums.

Poor Anto can't even speak properly and everyone says he is fading away; he just gets thinner and thinner. It breaks my heart to think about him.

There are some who would say it's his own fault and blame him for becoming a drug addict in the first place but I'm not angry at Anto, I blame the pushers who took his life and that of many others in the inner city. They took them in their prime, when they were young and hopeful and had the world at their feet. They ruined their lives for the sake of a few bob.

*chapter twenty-four*

ONE AFTERNOON I came home from the shops to find Aoife lying at the bottom of the stairs in the hallway. She was 12-years-old at the time and Johnny had beaten her up. I nearly died when I saw her lying in a pool of blood with a huge gash on her face and blood everywhere. One of the two chandeliers above her had fallen and there was glass all over the floor. At first I thought it must have dropped on top of her head and cut her face. She was wailing with the pain.

"Ahh, darlin'," I cried out, "What in God's name happened to you? Was it the chandelier Aoife, was it?"

I was kneeling on the ground with her head in my lap and there was so much blood it was all over her lovely, little face. We were both crying.

"It was him Ma," she managed to say in between sobs. She was overcome with anger and pain, and the sheer shock of all that had happened to her.

Johnny had attacked her because she answered him back. She had wanted to go out with her friends to play on the road, but he wouldn't let her. He told her she was grounded and sent her to her room for the afternoon. In a fit of anger she'd told him to "fuck off." That one remark had pushed him over the edge.

"Think you can talk to me like that. Do you?" he'd roared at her. And in the blink of an eyelid, he'd pulled a u-shaped, metal lock from his pocket. It was one he always carried with him, it fitted neatly into his palm and he used to wrap it around two of his fingers to keep it on. He had purposefully whacked his own daughter in the mouth with it.

She was on her way up the stairs at the time and he'd pulled her back by the hair and aimed at her mouth. The bastard.

It was bad enough beating me for years but only the lowest of the low attacks their own flesh and blood and this was no accident. Aoife had reeled with the pain, as she did one of the chandeliers had fallen on the ground beside her.

I helped Aoife into the car and took her to hospital where the gash on her upper lip was stitched. The doctor on duty at the time was a nice, gentle man. "Who did this to you?" he asked Aoife gently.

I was shocked by her response but proud of her too.

"My Da did it," she said defiantly.

The young doctor stepped back.

"Is this true?" he turned to me, and I could tell by his expression that he was shocked. I nodded painfully. I felt ashamed and guilty. I felt like it was my fault and perhaps part of me believed it was, after all, I'd married the man. What's more I should have been there to protect her. If I'd been there maybe he would have gone for me instead.

I loved my children so much I'd have taken a beating rather than see them hurt. The sick thing was that I knew Johnny so well and I knew this was his way of getting at me.

Aoife is now an adult. She still has that scar and it will be there for life. She's a beautiful, young woman but every time she looks in the mirror she's reminded of Johnny and all the pain he's put her through.

When the girls got a bit older they became interested in boys. They were still in their early teens and I wanted them to wait a few years before they had boyfriends but there was nothing I could do about it. I suspect they were subconsciously looking for a way out of their home life.

Aoife was the first to have a boyfriend. She was slim and dark and all the boys liked her. She was 14 when she fell for a young fella from around the corner—a quiet lad called Mark who was crazy about her. Johnny wasn't pleased of course.

"Tell those girls not to be going with lads," he used to say to me, as if it was my fault.

Mark seemed like a nice chap and I was pleased that Aoife had someone to depend on. He was only with us a few weeks when Johnny turned on him.

He came in drunk one afternoon and attacked poor Mark who was drinking tea in the kitchen.

"You think you're great, don't you?" he said to the poor lad, who was terrified out of his wits. "Think you're great going out with my daughter?"

I was upstairs with Aoife at the time and we could hear every word that was said downstairs. Then the kitchen door was closed shut.

"Quick Ma," said Aoife. "We've got to help Mark."

We carefully tiptoed down the stairs and stuck our head through the banisters, straining to hear what was going on.

There was a little window over the kitchen door and we could see through it. Johnny was sitting at the kitchen table with two carving knives in his hand. He seemed to be sharpening one with the other, he kept running one of them down the other blade, and he did it slowly but determinedly. Aoife was out of her mind with worry.

"Holy shit, he's going to kill Mark," she looked at me in terror. "What are we going to do?"

Mark was sitting opposite Johnny in a chair at the table and he looked terrified. My heart raced.

"Come on Aoife, let's go round the back and see if we can hear what they're saying," I whispered to my daughter.

The two of us went out the front door, closed it softly behind us and then we tiptoed around the side to the back garden where we crouched beside the door and tried to hear what was going on.

Johnny was taunting Mark, slagging him off and trying to undermine his confidence.

"You think Aoife loves you, don't you?" he said in a sneering voice. "She doesn't love you," he laughed mockingly. "She's just using you."

Mark said nothing.

"She doesn't give a shit about you. You're just a fuckin' eejit."

Johnny was in full flight now; ranting like there was no tomorrow and poor Mark didn't know how to react. Eventually he stood up, muttered something about going and walked out. Johnny just sat there, muttering to himself.

Mark got away without a beating that day and it wasn't long until Aoife left the house and moved into a flat with him.

My husband could be some bastard when he wanted to be. He was so clever too; he always picked on people who weren't able for him. Mark was a quiet, sensitive guy; the sort who wouldn't stand up to Johnny.

Molly's boyfriend however was another matter. She started going out with Keith about a year after Aoife met Mark. Molly was always a little bit tubby when she was young, and he was the first boyfriend she'd ever had. Keith was a feisty young fella who came from a similar background to her.

Although I worried about the girls getting attached so young and worried too that they could end up with violent husbands, I was glad they now had some form of protection from Johnny.

What's more it gave them hope of a happy future; hope was a quality that all of us lacked living with Johnny Smith. Although I had long ago given up hoping myself, I didn't want my girls to beaten down at such an early age. I wanted them to have the life I'd been denied.

*chapter twenty-five*

YOUNG FRANCES STILL lived at home with me back then. Out of all the girls she got away with the most. Johnny always had a soft spot for her and rarely hit her. She'd get upset when she saw him attack me but for some reason she'd forgive him afterwards and blame it on the drink.

"He's an alcoholic Ma," she'd say. "It's not his fault."

Her reaction would upset me but at the same time I knew how manipulative Johnny could be. She was torn between her parents.

The other two girls lived with their boyfriends nearby, but we were in regular contact. Most days they'd call around for tea.

A year after Aoife moved out she had a little boy. Molly also had a baby boy and I now had two lovely grandchildren and I was a proud grandmother.

The day after Molly was released from hospital, she and Aoife called in to see me. It was a sunny day and we were all standing outside the house that afternoon when Johnny arrived home. He was angry and drunk when he got out of the car. He'd recently bought it and he loved that car.

"What the fuck are you doing standing in the driveway with that child?" he roared at Aoife for no reason.

Then he spat in her face and the spit fell on to the baby whom she was holding in her arms. Johnny laughed and walked into the house.

Aoife said nothing. She was used to that sort of behaviour from her father. She could have let it pass but for some reason she lost her temper and took revenge that day. And what a revenge it was.

She wiped the spit off her face as she went inside and handed the baby to me.

"Mind him for a minute Ma," she said. Her face was full of anger. Then she grabbed a hammer from the press in the kitchen and ran back out into the driveway.

I'll never forget the look of determination on her face as she wielded that hammer—throwing it back and swinging it with all her might, she was poetry in motion.

First she smashed the side of Johnny's car. Smash, bang, the glass lay in pieces on the ground and the sound seemed to echo around the street. Like that, a group of kids appeared and stood at a distance watching her.

Then she wielded the hammer again, this time going for the front window of the car; the hammer came flying through the air and straight through the windscreen. The glass went everywhere—inside the car and all over the road. It lay scattered like shards of diamond, glinting in the sunlight.

The neighbours were talking now.

"What's she doing? Is she alright?" I could hear muffled voices and the sound of doors opening. More children appeared as if from nowhere, some had bicycles, they giggled and shrieked each time she smashed a window, enjoying the sheer drama of the whole scene.

I could tell by her face that each time she wielded that hammer and smashed through the glass of Johnny's precious car she felt a little freer. All those years of pent-up emotions, of anger and pain and fear were coming to a head and this was her way of expressing them. She had purpose in her aim as she went for the back window of the car and then the lights—first the back and then the front ones. She didn't stop until she had broken every piece of glass on the vehicle.

As she broke the last window, she dropped the hammer on the ground and suddenly broke into tears. She looked at me with a forlorn expression on her face. Just then a round of applause broke out among the kids on the street. They were clapping and cheering.

"Go on you mad thing," one cheeky, young fella shouted. "Will you do my car?"

Aoife laughed. We all laughed; we had to.

Just then Johnny appeared at the door. The look on his face was priceless as he stared at his beloved car. He was white with anger.

"You fuckin' bitch," he roared at Aoife. Then he ran and threw himself at her. He fell on top of her and they both fell to the ground.

He punched Aoife in the face with all his might and her screams echoed around the road. Even the kids were quiet. They stood and watched in amazement.

Just then however another car pulled up and this time it was Aoife's boyfriend Mark.

"Leave her alone you bastard," he roared at Johnny as he got out of the car and ran for him.

He was on Johnny's back now, scratching at his face and biting his ear. Johnny stood up and he fell backwards but Mark got to his feet and landed a punch right on Johnny's jaw. Johnny stood back, foaming at the mouth, and then he hit poor Mark and knocked him to the ground.

Aoife was still lying on the pavement and the fight between the two men had moved into the centre of the street by now. Johnny had the upper hand; he was beating poor Mark to a pulp.

Molly was standing watching the whole scene and she suddenly turned to me. There was panic in her voice.

"Ma what are we going to do? Da is going to kill Mark."

Suddenly she made a running jump at Johnny's back. He stood up and she fell back on to the concrete and screamed as she clutched her stomach. She had only been released from hospital the day before and the stitches from her caesarean section had yet to heal. I ran to her side. She lifted her jumper and there was blood and pus oozing out of her stomach; the stitches had burst.

I looked up and Mark was kicking the daylights out of Johnny who lay on the ground.

"You bastard," he shouted over and over again.

"Stop it Mark," Aoife was on her feet now. She ran to his side and pulled him away. The fight was over and Johnny lay on the ground, curled up in the foetal position with his hands over his head.

We had to call an ambulance that day. Poor Molly had to go to hospital to be restitched.

It was a hard price to pay but I don't think Aoife ever regretted wrecking the windows of his car. She still talks about it proudly to this day.

# PART THREE

*chapter twenty-six*

AFTER I TOOK the first overdose, I spent three days in hospital; they were three long days. After Johnny was thrown out he didn't come near me again. The girls came to see me and Helen and Fiona stopped by, but I still felt isolated. A hospital ward can be a very lonely place.

I felt mortified—ashamed and guilty. I felt like the most private part of my life had been exposed and I was raw and vulnerable.

The hospital staff were kind and sympathetic but not one of them brought the subject of Johnny up again. I think they didn't want to know. They were probably used to battered wives; no counselling service was offered to me despite the fact that I'd tried to kill myself and no one suggested I contact the guards.

I was relieved when they finally let me go home. I had no one to bring me back that day so I called a taxi.

It's funny how being away from a situation for a few days can make it seem clearer. As I sat in the back of the taxi, I stared out the window and my mind drifted back over the events of the past few years.

In the days before, as I lay in hospital, I'd been trying to pinpoint when exactly I stopped coping. I suppose I'd been trying to explain my attempt at killing myself.

As I sat in silence in the back of the car and looked out the window at the grey, urban landscape, it came flooding back to me. I wasn't taking in the housing estates with their row upon row of same-looking council houses, the burnt out cars lying abandoned in patches of littered, greenery or the lifeless look of the people I passed, I was thinking back to the night Johnny had raped me.

Of course he'd been drunk, he was always drunk but that night he was in a vicious mood, angry and belligerent. He'd wanted sex and for once I'd refused him. I was sick at the time; I had terrible pains in my stomach. I couldn't stand the thought of sleeping with him; I just couldn't bare it. I'd gone to bed early in the hope that maybe he'd leave me alone.

"Perhaps he'll come in and fall into bed, drunk out of his mind," I thought to myself. But no, Johnny wasn't tired that night.

I listened as he climbed the stairs and there was purpose in his step. By the time he reached the bedroom I was shaking with fear.

"Think you can fool me?" he slurred as he slammed the door.

"I know all your little tricks," he hiccuped loudly. "You're not asleep and I know it."

Then he jumped on to the bed and made a grab for my breast. I was angry now and upset. "Why should I have to give in to this beast of a man?" I thought. I sat up in the bed and pushed his arm away from me.

"No Johnny, you can fuck off, I'm not sleeping with you tonight. I'm not well. Just leave me alone."

But even as I said the words I knew I shouldn't have. He was furious, angry and determined.

"You're my wife and I'll fuck you if I want to," he roared at the top of his voice. I was terrified; I knew that he was capable of anything. I wanted to run but my body just froze with fear.

And then he was on top of me, pushing down on my body, heaving and groaning. I screamed at the top of my voice, using every ounce of energy and determination I possessed.

"No" my voice seemed to echo around the room and I thought that the whole neighbourhood must have heard me, but they didn't. Nobody heard my pitiful cry for help. And then he covered my mouth with his hand.

"You fucking bitch, how dare you deny me," he snarled. "I'll show you."

His dirty fingers were in my mouth and I thought I was going to suffocate or choke, but there was nothing I could do.

He grabbed both my arms with his other hand and held them over my head. I was pinned to the bed with him on top of me, pushing inside and the pain was horrific.

"You bastard," I wanted to scream out loud. I felt like tearing his hair out and gouging his eyes with my fingers. I wanted to kill him, but I couldn't. He was on top of me and I couldn't move. Then he came inside me and I wanted to die.

This wasn't about sex or love or alcoholism, this was an act of power and nothing else. He wanted to control me and I was powerless to stop him.

Afterwards I lay whimpering in the bed beside him, while he rolled over and snored for Ireland. My whole body ached and I felt dirty, filthy, the lowest of the low.

"If this is living," I thought to myself. "Then I don't want to do it anymore."

But worse was yet to come. Within a year, I found I was pregnant again. I was utterly shocked when my GP told me. Ever since I'd had young Frances I'd been on the pill. I was still on it at the time and I just couldn't understand how I could possibly be pregnant.

Looking back however I suffered from chronic diarrhoea, which I have no doubt was a direct result of the constant fear in which I lived. The pill must have passed through me at some stage.

I was so shocked when I discovered I was pregnant that I went into a state of denial. I started laughing hysterically when the doctor told me and I left the surgery that day denying the truth to myself. For years the only thing that had kept me going was the knowledge that I could one day leave my husband.

"Once young Frances reaches 16-years of age," I'd think to myself, "I'm out of here. I'm gone out that door, never to return."

The irony was I'd nearly reached that stage. The girls were getting older, Frances was the only one still at home. All of them were becoming more independent and they needed me less and less.

I didn't want another baby. The thought of having to change nappies and look after a child again killed me, but more than anything I didn't want this child because it meant I was trapped; chained to Johnny for at least another 16 years and I just couldn't face the prospect.

For a few weeks, I blocked it out of my mind and convinced myself that I wasn't pregnant. I didn't tell anyone including Johnny. But little by little the realisation dawned on me and I had to tell my husband. He acted like it was no big deal. He was cold and aloof as always. I suspected that he was secretly pleased at the prospect.

I confronted him a few nights later, I broke down and told him there was no way I was having the baby. I wanted an abortion. To my surprise Johnny agreed.

That afternoon I looked up the Yellow Pages and phoned the Well Woman Centre. It was around the time of one of the abortion referendums in Ireland and they told me to get hold of a Northern Ireland phone book and to ring a number there. I remember going into the GPO in the centre of the city and searching for a number.

Eventually I found one, I took down the details, but I never rang them. It didn't take long for Johnny to change his mind. That evening he came back drunk.

"You think you're having an abortion do you?" he roared. "There's no way I'm letting you kill our child."

I knew he didn't care about the child. It would only be another one for him to beat up for God's sake. He knew he had me trapped and there was no way out.

Helen came to visit me the next day. She knew all about Johnny by now so I had nothing to hide from her. Johnny didn't like me seeing her but she insisted on calling at the house and there was nothing he could do about it. At that stage I didn't care what he thought, I knew he'd beat me anyway. I wept bitter tears as I sat in the front room and told her the news.

"Frances why are you crying? Sure it's great that you're having another baby. It's never a bad thing," she said gently, trying to comfort me.

"You don't understand Helen," I shook my head and wiped my nose with a tissue.

"It means I'm stuck here, stuck with Johnny forever."

Helen knew my situation was bad but nobody could quite understand it unless they'd lived through it. She probably thought I was over reacting.

I realise now that in the weeks that followed, I wasn't thinking straight. All I could think about was the pregnancy and after a while I slipped back into a state of denial. I didn't eat properly at the time and the bump on my stomach was very small so nobody noticed it.

Helen was worried about me. She told me afterwards that Johnny had turned around to her one day when I was out of the room.

"She thought she was going to leave me?" he'd said. "She thought she was going to walk out on her husband? I showed her. She's never going anywhere without me."

The nine months leading up to the birth of the child passed in a blur. For years I had drifted along with my head buried in the sand, refusing to face reality.

Now I was beginning to realise the truth about my life and I was in a state of profound despair. It was as if all the years of suffering had finally caught up on me.

When the baby arrived, I was totally unprepared. I hadn't bought any baby clothes. I didn't even have an overnight bag packed for when I went to hospital. But Helen was great at the time. For months she'd been begging me to face up to the situation.

"You're going to have a baby Frances, you're pregnant," she'd say to me and I'd laugh at the notion. Then she'd get angry.

"It's not funny Frances, you have to start looking after yourself."

Johnny drove me to the hospital on the day I was to have the baby. We had another little girl and she was born perfectly healthy. I called her Caitríona.

Despite the fact that I'd denied I was pregnant and had been dreading the baby's birth, once they placed the tiny little thing in my arms I loved her as much, if not more, than all the others. She was cute and adorable and as her little hand clasped around my finger, I thanked God for this beautiful child.

Fiona came to visit me in the recovery room after the birth. She later told me I looked like death warmed up and she'd been very worried. The birth had taken a lot out of me.

I had to stay in hospital for two weeks to recover. They gave me a blood transfusion because I was anaemic. I was very run-down at the time.

*chapter twenty-seven*

THE DAY I was released from hospital I called into Helen's house with the baby, on the way home. I felt very weak while I was there but I put it down to recovering from the birth. Helen drove me home that day and I went to bed.

The following day however I still felt weak and I had to lie down for the day. At one stage my temperature climbed so high, I was delirious.

That evening Johnny was in the pub and young Frances was off somewhere with her friends. I lay awake in the house with Caitríona in the cot at the end of the bed.

From the moment I took Caitríona home, all the girls had doted on her. Johnny hadn't shown much interest but then he'd long ago lost interest in his

197

family. All he cared about now was drinking and robbing to feed his alcoholism. He was drinking more than ever. He'd wake up with his hands shaking and they wouldn't be steady until he'd downed his first drink in the early house. He didn't even try to stay off the booze anymore, it was as if he'd given in and resigned himself to a life of alcoholism.

That night as I lay in bed, my temperature climbed so high I was convinced that I could see a figure standing beside the cot and in my fevered state I thought it was my grandmother; who I had stayed with as a child. I could see her standing there; her hair was white and her features looked exactly as they had in real life. She was beckoning to me. Funnily enough I didn't feel afraid. Perhaps I wanted to die.

I woke up the next morning and the fever had passed. I was weak as a kitten and had to be rushed back into hospital. The doctors told me there was an abscess on my stomach. It had to be removed but I was too weak to undergo an operation.

They kept me in hospital for a week before they removed the abscess and the operation was horrendous. They had to freeze my stomach and then they put a tube in to suction it out. I was given a local anesthetic but I could feel everything and the pain was excruciating.

Johnny sat outside the operating room playing the dutiful husband. I remember when they wheeled me out on the trolley afterwards, he was standing there.

"Jesus, they must have heard your screams in Cork," was all he said.

The following year I found myself constantly ill and in and out of hospital. I had severe problems with my bowels and they also discovered a cyst on one of my ovaries, which could have required a hysterectomy. As it happens, I didn't need one but they removed the cyst and it was a big operation.

I seemed to be always recovering from operations at the time. It was as if my body had given up. What's more I went into a deep, post-natal depression after the birth.

I suppose I was having a form of a nervous breakdown without realising it. The beatings were worse than ever. At one stage a doctor pulled me aside.

"Frances can I talk to you," he said gently and I knew what was coming. "The nurses have been talking," he looked me straight in the eye. "Frances you have to tell me, are you being abused by your husband?"

I was taken aback. In all the years I'd been in different hospitals around Dublin I had never been asked outright about the abuse I suffered. No member of staff had ever volunteered to help me and I honestly didn't know how to react. I'd told them about Aoife the time she cut her lip and I couldn't cover up for Molly when Johnny had hit her over the head with a saucepan but I had never admitted the abuse I suffered myself.

Back then I was so vulnerable, so tense, so afraid; I just couldn't do it. I couldn't tell the doctor the truth.

"He'll kill me as soon as I go home," I thought. "Johnny Smith will kill me stone dead."

But more than anything I felt ashamed. I blushed profusely at the attention the doctor was giving me. I didn't want him to know the truth and I felt acutely embarrassed.

"No doctor," I shook my head as I stared at the ground. I couldn't meet his eyes. "Of course I'm not being abused," I pretended to be shocked. "As I said, I fell down the stairs."

The young doctor was annoyed with me.

"I can't help you unless you tell me the truth Frances," he said.

I said nothing and I kept my head bent and eventually he left the room. He never brought the subject up again.

All the time I was in hospital and afterwards recovering I couldn't have managed without Molly. She took over the housework and looked after the baby when I took to my bed. The other girls helped out too and between all of us we managed.

Aoife and Molly still called around every day and we remained as close as ever.

Frances was a bit different to the other girls. She was too young to remember all of the violence and she had always been Johnny's favourite.

On one occasion Johnny came in drunk from the pub and there was no dinner made for him. I'd been feeling sick all day and it was all I could do to lift myself off the couch and answer the door to him. He'd forgotten his key.

He strode into the kitchen and sat purposefully at the kitchen table as he usually did.

"Where's my dinner?" he demanded. "Johnny, I've been awful sick today. I just wasn't able to make it. I'm terrible sorry. The girls have been out all day too. I was hoping one of them might do it."

"So what have you been doing?" he asked and I knew he wasn't pleased.

"I've been lying down," I said and the words almost choked me. I knew what was coming next and I couldn't take the tension. I grabbed a kitchen chair and sat down. My head felt dizzy. I hadn't eaten a thing all day because I was sick.

"You what?" he roared at me in disgust. "You lazy bitch. I've been out working all day and you don't even have a meal ready for me when I come home. I'll show you."

Before he got out of the seat I felt an overwhelming desire to use the toilet. I stood up and made a run for the stairs. I got as far as the hallway before he pulled me back by the hair and a big clump came off in his hand. My scalp stung but I didn't care, all I could think of was reaching the toilet.

Then he grabbed me again. This time by the arm, he swung me around and punched me in the jaw. I fell to the floor and he began kicking me in the groin. I screamed with the pain.

I tried to hold it but it was no good. Suddenly my bowels opened up, it happened partly from fear and partly because I was unwell. The stench was unbearable. Johnny looked down at the ground and took a step back. I was mortified. I wanted the ground to open up and swallow me at that moment.

"What's that?" he said looking at the ground. Then he lifted his head.

"You filthy bitch," he screamed. "Look what you've gone and done now."

He leaned down and threw me another punch in the face before he walked off. I was left a snivelling mess lying in my own faeces.

After that beating, I tried to commit suicide again. Once more it was a failed attempt. This time around I didn't even give the drugs time to kick in. I panicked and phoned an ambulance myself, and then I was rushed to the hospital where they pumped my stomach before I lost consciousness.

It's a horrible feeling to have your stomach pumped. They stick a long tube down your throat and deep into the stomach. It feels sore and very un-comfortable. Then they start to bring up this horrible, tar-like muck from inside you. Just to look at it makes you want to retch but you can't because you have a tube in your mouth. The pump goes on and on for what seems like an eternity until the entire contents of your stomach have been emptied into a bucket beside you.

Believe me it's not pleasant and you feel totally drained and slightly spaced. I remember lying in the hospital bed afterwards. I felt very low—utterly ashamed and humiliated. The doctors and nurses were polite but I could see they had little sympathy for me.

One of them phoned Johnny and he arrived to take me home that evening. Helen had to come in to visit and was helping me get dressed at the time.

"What the fuck is she doing here?" said Johnny when he arrived into the hospital. "Get her out of here before I throw her out," he roared at me. "I can dress my own wife."

I had to ask poor Helen to leave.

There was silence as we drove. I knew he was angry with me for trying to take my own life again but there was an air of triumph about him too. For years he'd been telling me I was mad.

"I'm not the one with the problem," he used to say. "It's you, you're crazy".

Now I was proving him right; I was living out his insults. I had reached an all-time low in that two-year period. The beatings were more and more frequent back then and he was getting more vicious too. Once the baby was born I realised that I had to get away from him somehow before he killed us all.

After my second suicide attempt, first Molly and then Aoife followed suit and tried to kill themselves.

They both took overdoses as I had. It makes me feel guilty that they followed my example but neither succeeded and I honestly don't think they wanted to die. It was before they both moved out and I think each of them had reached the same level of despair as I had.

Molly was the first to do it. It happened one night after a fight with Johnny. She was sobbing uncontrollably afterwards and she went upstairs to clean her face. She didn't come down for a long time but I didn't think much of it. I knew she was upset and I thought I should leave her alone. When she did appear in the front room she was pale as a ghost.

"Oh Ma," she screamed at me. "Ma, I've gone and done it. I'm after taking a load of painkillers. I feel sick Ma, what am I going to do?"

I got her into the car as quickly as I could and rushed her to the hospital. Thank God we got her in time. They were able to pump her stomach and she lived to tell the tale.

Then a short while later Aoife did the same thing. It was as if once I'd done it, suicide had suddenly become an option. I found Aoife on the bathroom floor one night and I rushed her to hospital.

Neither of the girls ever attempted it again.

"Don't do it," I warned them both afterwards. "Why should you let him ruin your life? If you do, then he has won."

I should have taken my own advice however. In that two-year period I took five overdoses in total and each time in a state of absolute despair. Johnny was drinking like there was no tomorrow and he was continuously violent and belligerent. He became impossible to live with and I just didn't know what else to do. I'd given up.

After each attempt, the doctors in the hospital would question me as to why I tried to kill myself. I'd lie; tell them I was depressed. I couldn't admit the truth. On the second last attempt, they sent to see a psychiatrist in the hospital.

"What made you want to kill yourself Mrs. Smith?" he asked me.

I simply hung my head and told him I'd been severely depressed. He told me I needed a rest and recommended that I spend two weeks in a psychiatric hospital.

When I came home and told the Johnny he went mad.

"There's no way you're going to a fucking mental home," he screamed at me.

He knew I would have been happy to escape his abuse for two weeks.

"But Johnny I need to go," I begged him. "It's only two weeks and then I'll be back."

"The answer is 'No,'" he roared at me and I didn't try to argue any more.

My last attempt at suicide was the worst. Molly found me on the floor of the bedroom and I was rushed to hospital by ambulance. After they had pumped my stomach I was in such a bad way that my heart stopped momentarily and they had to resuscitate me. I was in intensive care at the time and the doctor told my family I wouldn't pull through. Helen was in terrible state. She phoned Johnny to tell him I was dying. He was in the pub.

I remember lying on the operating table at the time and thinking,

"Well this is it. I'm finally going to die."

I'd come so close to death on numerous occasions that it now felt like an old friend and I was ready; I'd had enough.

My life flashed before my eyes and I felt removed from it, as if I was seeing the events of the last few years at a distance. I saw my father walking through the inner city on his way home from work on a sunny evening. He was smiling at me. Then I was standing in the doorway of our first flat, I had Aoife in my arms and she was just a baby. There was an image of young Frances chasing a butterfly in the back garden when she was a toddler and Molly running after her. And Anto as a teenager on a bike before he had AIDS and my mother standing talking to my grandmother.

Then I saw myself sitting on the back of Johnny's motorbike at the age of 13. I was laughing and the wind was blowing in my hair as we sped along the street. All those images and more flashed, one after the other, in my mind and I suddenly felt at peace.

Then the thought occurred to me that if I died, Johnny would have won and with that realisation I became angry and the anger gave me energy and made me want to fight back. Suddenly the images disappeared and something deep inside me made me gasp for air. I fought back with every ounce of energy in my body.

And as I sucked the air into my lungs, everything seemed clearer, as if a cloud had lifted. I knew then I had to get away. I was going to leave Johnny Smith for once and for all.

*chapter twenty-eight*

I LEFT THINGS as they were for a few days after I returned from the hospital and then I went to the guards. My GP had instructed me to take photographs of my body the last time Johnny had beaten me up and although many of the scars had healed I still had the photographs. I was terrified that Johnny might find them so I had hidden them under a loose floorboard in the girl's bedroom.

I pulled them out one night when he was in the pub. They were horrible and it killed me to look at them. I felt so ashamed. At the same time I knew that I had to act quickly and inform the guards.

The young guard in the local station was sympathetic. It was difficult to talk about the years of abuse but I told him everything.

I was determined to get rid of Johnny and even shame couldn't stop me. The guard showed me how to fill out a form and sent me to the courts where I got a barring order against my husband. The judge was a nice, gentle man and he gave it to me without a problem.

When I showed the barring order to Johnny that evening he went crazy. He was sitting in the front room at the time and he jumped off the couch and locked the door. He always made a point of locking the door or pulling the phone lines out when he was going to beat me up. Johnny planned his attacks.

Then he grabbed the barring order out of my hands. He read it for a few minutes and then he grabbed me by the hair and tried to shove it down my throat.

"You bitch," he screamed. "How dare you!"

I couldn't breathe. I thought I was going to suffocate. Helen had given me a lift home from the court and she was in the kitchen at the time but she couldn't get in because he'd locked the door. She could hear him screaming at me and she banged on the door. "Frances, are you alright?" she shouted out but I couldn't answer.

Johnny beat me black and blue that evening and left me on the ground, crying. He was furious that I'd dared to stand up to him. Afterwards he went to bed. When he'd stomped upstairs Helen came running in and picked me off the floor.

"Oh Frances, what has he done to you?" she said and now she too was crying.

I was in terrible pain. My whole body ached and he had hurt my throat so badly that I could hardly speak. My sister knelt down on the ground beside me and hugged me. We sat like that for ages, the two of us sobbing.

When I did finally pull myself together, I decided I had to get out before he woke up. We tiptoed around the house, gathering bits and pieces of clothing and shoving them into a small suitcase with Helen helping me. My heart was racing the whole time and all I could think about was getting away. Then I took Caitríona in my arms and young Frances by the hand.

Helen's son was also there at the time and he came with us. "Come on now," I whispered to young Frances. "We've got to run."

The five of us managed to get out of the house quietly without waking Johnny and we ran down the road together.

It was raining that day and we got soaked, but we didn't care. We literally ran as fast as our legs could carry us. I was too scared to even look over my shoulder.

We'd got a few hundred yards up the road when I heard a car behind us and turned around to look. It was Johnny. He'd obviously heard us leave the house and now he was following us.

"Quick," I shouted to Helen. "Get that bus."

I pointed at a bus, which had just pulled up beside us. We made a dash for the bus, me with Caitríona in my arms. We made it. I fumbled for the fare as the bus pulled off. I watched out the back window as Johnny's car pulled over to the side of the street and I heaved a sigh of relief. We'd escaped.

I had nowhere to go to at that time, Johnny knew Helen was with me and he'd come looking for us if we went to her house, so I decided I'd have to level with Johnny's brother Brian.

I'd ask him if we could stay there until I figured out a plan. We arrived at his house late that evening. We had to get another bus from town. Young Frances was tired and Caitríona was crying.

Brian nearly died when he opened the front door. I hadn't seen him or his wife for years. Johnny's family knew he was an alcoholic but none of them knew the full extent of his drinking and the violence. I told Brian everything and he was very shocked. He agreed that the two girls and myself could stay with him for a few days. I was relieved. At least we had somewhere to sleep that night.

It was only a matter of time however until Johnny found out where we were. He came banging on the door two days later. Of course he was drunk out of his mind. Brian refused to let him in; he opened the door and told him to go away.

"You're drunk, Johnny and Fran doesn't want to see you."

Johnny had to leave. He wasn't able to stand up to his brother.

We stayed with Brian, his wife and three kids for a week and a half. They were very kind to us, but I knew I couldn't stay there for much longer. It was small house and we all barely fitted into it. Young Frances was still in secondary school and it meant she had to get two buses to school. Besides we only had a few pieces of clothing with us and I had no money.

I went to visit my father and while I was there Johnny phoned. He was sober for once and reasonable on the phone.

"Please come home," he begged. "I promise you it won't happen again."

I gave in. I really didn't have a choice in the matter. We would have been destitute, living on the streets and no matter how bad things were at home at least we had a roof over out head. I returned home but of course nothing changed.

A few weeks later Johnny beat me up very badly. This time I decided to go back to the guards and they persuaded me to get him charged with assault.

I had to go to Kilmainham District Court to give evidence against him.

I'll never forget the morning of the trial. I arrived and two of his mates were waiting outside the door of the courtroom. I recognised them both, they were hard men with reputations.

Before I could get past them, one grabbed me by the arm and pulled me aside.

"If you give evidence against Johnny, I'll shoot you," he whispered in my ear. "You won't walk out of that courtroom alive Frances Smith."

He was a huge man with a firm grip and I was terrified. I didn't know if he had a gun or not but people used to say he carried a blade which he used to slice open people's faces.

I was shaking with fear when I walked into that courtroom but I was defiant. I didn't care if they killed me; I was going to give evidence against Johnny Smith come hell or high water. I sat down and waited to be called to the stand. I looked straight ahead and tried to remain calm. But the two thugs kept turning their heads to stare at me.

A young guard was standing nearby and he must have noticed what was happening. He came over.

"Mrs. Smith, are these men bothering you?" he said politely.

"Yes, guard they are," I replied.

Then he asked them to leave the courtroom. One of the men glared at me as he stood up. He didn't have to speak; I could see the anger in his face. Johnny was sitting at the other side of the courtroom. Suddenly he also stood up and left as well.

When the case was called, there was no sign of Johnny. He'd disappeared. There was no need for me to give evidence. The judge ordered that a warrant be issued for his arrest.

Shortly afterwards he was picked up for another crime but he was sent to a rehabilitation centre for men with drug and alcohol addictions.

He was there a couple of weeks and for the whole time he plagued me with phone calls.

The children felt sorry for him and visited him a few times.

Before he was picked up by the guards, I'd been asking him to sign the house over to me. It was in both our names at the time.

Johnny told Aoife to tell me that he'd sign it over if I agreed to drop the assault charges against him.

"Tell your Ma, I'll sign over the house and leave her alone. I'll do anything if she gets me out of here," he said to Aoife, who promptly relayed the message back to me.

I agreed to his request. If the house was in my name then I could sell it and escape from Johnny once and for all. I should have known better however. As soon as he was released he refused to sign it over. What's more he was round at the house, demanding that I let him come back.

This time there was nothing I could do to stop him. I tried complaining to the guards again but they took me less seriously than before because I'd dropped the charges against him the first time.

In the following two years I rang them regularly about my husband. In that time, I got five barring orders against Johnny but they weren't worth the paper they were written on.

On one occasion I left with the kids and went to live with Helen. Of course Johnny came home that evening and was furious. He rang my mobile but I turned it off and refused to answer it. The next evening we were sitting watching television in Helen's house. Aoife and Molly were there too and we were all squashed into the small front room with Helen.

I was sitting in an armchair with Molly at my feet when suddenly I heard a noise behind me. Before I could even turn around, I felt a hand clasp my hair from behind and a knife was placed at my throat. I panicked but I couldn't move my head. Then I heard his voice.

"Think you're great don't you, leaving your husband who's stood by you all these years?"

He was drunk; I could smell the alcohol off him.

"Didn't I always tell you, you'll die before you ever leave me."

I could only see ahead of me and Molly was on her feet now.

"Leave her alone Da, leave her fuckin' alone," she screamed, and then Helen spoke.

"Johnny, put the knife down, put the knife down slowly Johnny."

The tension in the air was tangible.

Helen lived in a flat and in order to get in, he must have glided the front door with a credit card, then climbed five flights of stairs and glided the front door of her home. He did it in complete silence, none of us heard him coming.

Suddenly Molly stood up and went for him, Johnny's hand slipped and I thought for a second he'd slit my throat. I screamed but no, the knife had fallen to the floor. Quick as a shot however he'd picked it up and when Molly went to grab him he got behind her and held it to her face.

"Think she's pretty do you?" he directed his comments at me. "Well she won't be very pretty when I've finished with her. If you don't come back with me now, she's going to get it. I'm going to slash her pretty little face in two and it will be your fault."

I was distraught. I didn't know what to do. I couldn't believe Johnny was willing to slash his own daughter's face.

"Okay Johnny," I broke down. "I'll come home with you. I'll do anything you want. Just please leave Molly alone," I begged him.

"You'll come home now?" he questioned me further.

"Yes," I screamed. "Yes. I'll come this minute. Just put the knife down, please Johnny. Don't hurt her."

He paused for a second, enjoying his victory and the momentary power he possessed.

"Okay then," he dropped the knife.

Molly fell to her knees and began sobbing uncontrollably.

"Right so," my husband turned to me.

"It's nine o'clock now and you'd better be in that house when I get home tonight."

He walked out of the room and into the hallway.

"I'll see you when I get home," he called after him as he jumped down the steps.

I had no choice but to return and he beat me black and blue that night.

On another occasion when I stormed out with the kids we went to my father's house. He was getting older and his health wasn't the best. He recently had open-heart surgery.

Da took us in and said we could stay for as long as we wanted to. I told him I was leaving Johnny and he didn't seem shocked. He had heard about how Johnny treated me from Helen and Fiona. I don't think he ever knew the full extent of the situation however and it was probably better that he didn't. I knew it would just worry him.

The night after I arrived in my father's house we were sitting in the front room when suddenly there was a sound outside. It sounded like breaking glass. I ran into the hallway to see a sledge hammer coming through the front door.

The stained glass panes were broken and the frame of the door was being chopped to pieces with the hammer. Of course it was Johnny. Who else would it be? Young Frances was with me at the time and she ran after me into the hall.

"Jesus Ma," she said. "It's Da and he's not very happy Ma."

I had to go home that time too because he threatened to kill us with the sledgehammer if we didn't go. My poor father was in a terrible state. He'd never seen Johnny as bad and he was terrified out of his wits. What's more, he was worried for our safety.

"Will you be alright love?" he looked at me with a fearful expression.

"Don't worry Da. I'll be okay," I blatantly lied knowing well that Johnny would beat me up as soon as I got home. I didn't want to worry my father because of his health. The poor man didn't need to worry about us on top of everything else.

*chapter twenty-nine*

AROUND THAT TIME I sensed something was up with Johnny. For years you could always set your clock by him. He'd be gone early in the morning, he'd take the girls to school then you wouldn't see him until the afternoon when he'd bring them back. He'd come back about the same time each evening but in the last few months he'd started to stay out late and come in at odd times.

One night he arrived in at four o'clock in the morning. He woke me up as he came in the bedroom door.

"Where the fuck were you?"

I sat up in bed.

"Oh, I was too drunk to come home. I fell asleep in the car, parked in a car park."

I smelt a rat immediately. I'd seen Johnny drive when he was so drunk he couldn't even stand, and being drunk had never stopped him coming home before. At the same time I thought maybe I was being paranoid.

"Sure where would he possibly be?" I thought in all innocence. But there were other signs that something strange was a foot. He had become over-protective of his mobile phone.

I remember one day he was lying on the couch, drunk when it rang. He jumped up immediately.

"Don't answer that," he warned. I wasn't going to answer it anyway but I was taken aback at his reaction. He was very on edge.

Another night we'd had a fight and I was in the front bedroom, crying my eyes out. He'd gone into the girls' room to make a phone call. Aoife and Molly were staying over and he thought they were asleep at the time but they weren't.

They told me the next day that they'd heard him talking to a woman. They couldn't make out what she was saying but they suspected it was a female voice. I still wasn't convinced that Johnny could be having an affair.

"Sure it was probably Paul's wife," I said. Paul was one of Johnny's mates. Looking back however why would he have been talking to his mate's wife in the small hours of the morning? It didn't make sense.

Then there were times when we'd fight in the middle of the night and he'd disappear. In all the years I'd known him he had never done that before. I still refused to believe Johnny could be unfaithful. My sisters backed me up.

"There's no way Johnny would ever have an affair Frances," Helen shook her head when I told her. "He's just not the type."

Fiona agreed.

"No, you're imagining it Fran," she said. "Sure he rants for hours about other men and how they have affairs outside of marriage. He hates women too; he won't enter a barber's shop if there's a woman working there. Johnny would never be unfaithful. Anyway who would have him?" she added.

Then we all laughed and I put the idea out of my head. Eventually the truth came out.

It was Robbie, a friend of Johnny's, who finally told me the facts.

We were sitting in a bar one evening. Johnny was deep in conversation with Robbie, and I was talking to Robbie's sister. When she got up to go the toilet I overheard some of the conversation between the two men. I didn't mean to listen, but I couldn't help it.

"If I had what you have Johnny," I heard Robbie say, "There's no way I'd do that."

"What do you mean?" said Johnny.

"Well you've a gorgeous wife and four lovely kids, sure what do you want to go and do that for?"

I knew then that something was up and I was determined to find out the truth, but it wasn't the time or the place. Those remarks went round and round in my head for days afterwards.

Although I had caught Johnny chatting up two dolly birds at Butlins years ago I had never seen him with another woman since, and I honestly believed he would never have an affair. He often used to say to me, "You'd never be with another man. Sure you wouldn't! I'd never go with another woman."

Shortly after that I was in the same bar with Johnny, Robbie and Fiona.

When Johnny went to the toilet I turned to Robbie.

"I need to know the truth Robbie. Is Johnny seeing somebody else?"

Robbie was sitting at the bar. He stared at the ground for a few moments and there was silence. I waited with baited breath. Then he looked at me. His voice was grave.

"Fran," he paused, "Do you know Polo?"

This was a nickname for a mate of Johnny's who lived across the road.

"He's with Polo's sister Sarah."

I couldn't speak with the shock. Maybe I should have seen it coming, call me a fool but I didn't. I sat there with my head spinning for a few moments, and then I got up. I had to get out of that bar before Johnny returned. I knew I couldn't face him without him knowing that I knew, and I could never let on that

222

Robbie had told me. He would have killed Robbie outright.

"Thank you Robbie," I managed to say and then I made a run for the door.

I ran all the way home, crying as I ran. I wasn't sure why I was running; I just wanted to get home as quickly as possible.

When Robbie had said Polo, I'd presumed it must have been the daughter in the family who was about 18 at the time, but later I found out it was actually the mother and not the daughter. She's in her fifties and older than Johnny. That was the nail in the coffin. I couldn't believe Johnny would betray me for an older woman.

Still, I didn't confront Johnny with the truth. I told the girls, and Helen and Fiona, but I had no evidence to back up the allegations. I bided my time, waiting for the truth to come out.

Shortly after that I went away for a weekend with Johnny and his mate Vinny. There was a hurling final in Galway and they were going to "work". I remember sitting in the hotel in Galway when I got a phone call from Molly.

"Ma, it's Molly. Where's Da?" she said.

"He's sitting here beside me darlin'," I said to Molly. "Is everything alright?" I had left Caitríona who was still a baby with Molly and Aoife for the weekend.

"Everything is grand Ma, I just thought I'd ring to check," said Molly but I knew from her voice she was worried about something.

I needed to speak to her, but I wanted to do it in private and there was no way Johnny would let me out of his sight.

The next morning I got out of bed early. Leaving Johnny behind me snoring loudly, I went down stairs to use the hotel phone.

"Aoife, it's Ma, I couldn't talk yesterday but I just wanted to check everything is okay love?" She couldn't talk at the time.

"Everything's fine Ma, but could you ring back in half an hour?" she said.

About an hour later I'd just finished breakfast with Johnny. He disappeared to buy a newspaper and I thought, "Right, this is my chance."

I used the mobile this time. Aoife answered.

"Is Da with you?" she asked and I told her he was gone to buy a paper.

"Are you sitting down Ma?" I said I was. "Well a young child came to the door last night with an envelope, she'd been sent by a woman who was standing on the road watching her. The child handed in the envelope and I opened it Ma," said Aoife her voice shaking.

"Inside was a bunch of keys belonging to Da and a letter. The letter said the keys had been left in the woman's flat two nights before."

Supposedly she'd heard him talking to me on the phone one night and as a result she'd thrown him out of her flat. She'd left her phone number on the end of the page for me to ring her.

I knew then I had to face the truth. There was no doubt about it; Johnny Smith was having an affair. There was silence from my end of the phone as the truth gradually sank in.

"Are you alright Ma?" said Aoife, her voice was worried.

I was sitting in the lobby of the hotel, crying my eyes out at that stage.

"I'm alright love," I sniffled down the phone. "Don't worry about me."

But she was worried.

"Ma, don't say anything to him down there, he'll only get drunk and beat you up."

I knew better however.

"Don't worry love, I won't," I said as I put down the phone.

I felt shattered. All those years I'd put up with beatings, and they had been worse than ever recently, and now on top of it all, he'd gone and had an affair. I resolved not to mention it to him immediately, but as soon as he came back he saw my tears and started questioning me.

"Jesus Christ, what's wrong with you now?"

I could feel the blood rising in my cheeks then and I just couldn't hold back the words.

"I know Johnny, I know you're having an affair with that woman, Sarah," I spat the words out and I was defiant and angry. I didn't care what the consequences were I had to confront him.

"What?"

He acted like I was mad; denied the allegation completely.

"That knacker? Sure what would I be doing with her?" he said implying that I was paranoid and over-possessive.

I walked away from him then. Aoife had given me the woman's phone number and I had to hear it from her own mouth. I stepped outside and phoned her on the mobile. My hands were shaking as I dialled the number.

"Hello," I said hesitantly. "Is that Sarah?"

Her voice was coarse and deep. She sounded like she'd smoked too many cigarettes in her lifetime.

"Yeah, who's that?" she replied.

I took a deep breath.

"It's Fran Smith," I said.

There was silence on the other end. When she did speak she told me everything; how they'd been seeing each other for months, how he told her he was going to leave me because I was mad, how he'd wanted to leave me for years but couldn't because of the children. There was an air of triumph in her tone.

It may sound ridiculous but even then I didn't quite believe he was having an affair.

"Maybe she's lying," I thought to myself. "Maybe she's the mad one?"

Johnny had denied it emphatically and I still believed that perhaps it was all just a vicious rumour.

"How do I know you're not making this up?" I asked the woman.

"Well," she paused for a second. "I have a photo of him on top of my television," she said.

"It was one of the two of you in the Canary Islands a few years ago. I tore it in half and kept the piece with him in it. If you don't believe me you can come round and see for yourself."

I knew that photograph well. It was taken one time when Johnny had insisted on taking me to the Canary Islands for my birthday a few years ago. I hadn't wanted to go but as usual I had no choice. He'd spent most of the holiday drunk and I couldn't relax because I was afraid of what he was going to do next. It was one long nightmare and I was glad to get home after a week.

Johnny looked well in the photo. He was standing by the pool at the time and he had a bottle of beer in his hand. I, on the other hand, looked completely miserable. The woman offered to meet me and show me the photograph and I agreed.

*chapter thirty*

I CONFRONTED JOHNNY with the details as soon as I put down the phone. I was furious. It was bad enough that he'd been cheating on me, but worse still that he couldn't even admit it to my face. We drove back to Dublin with his friend Vinny in the car. When I reached the house that night, I told Johnny that I'd arranged to meet the woman. He was still denying the affair.

"If it's not true then why don't you come with me?" I said to him.

"I'm not coming with you," he said.

"Right so, I'll get her to come here," I said. Johnny walked out of the house.

"I'm going to drop Vinny home."

I knew he wouldn't return.

About an hour later I got a phone call. It was Vinny.

"We're sitting here in the hotel bar and he wants to have a word with you."

"About what?" I said.

"About your woman, Sarah."

Before I could get a word in, Vinny added, "Now don't start screaming, the truth is he was with her, but he never slept with her, he only ever slept on her couch."

Of course I knew that wasn't true. Vinny suggested that Johnny could come up to collect me in the car so that the three of us could go down to the hotel and have a chat about it. I agreed.

Johnny arrived and we drove to the hotel in silence. Then the three of us sat at the bar while Johnny denied he had ever slept with the woman.

"I swear on Caitríona's eyesight that I never slept with her," he tried to convince me. "When you first threw me out, I stayed in a mate's house for a while but it wasn't clean and I didn't like it. Sarah offered me her couch and I accepted it a few times. That's all I swear, I swear on my Caitríona's life."

I looked at him with complete disgust.

"What kind of fool do you think I am?" I said but he continued to deny the affair and by the time we left the hotel bar he was rotten drunk.

He begged me to stay that night and in the end I agreed. I'd had a long day and I was exhausted. I knew if I refused he'd beat me up, so I let him stay out of fear as long as he slept on the couch. All I wanted at that stage was to sleep. I felt completely gutted and lacking in energy.

I wasn't in the bed two minutes however until I felt him climb in beside me and touch me on the arm. I was furious.

"Get out of the bed this minute because you're making me sick," I roared at him.

"Do you really expect me to have sex with you and you after sleeping with another woman? Are you out of your mind?"

He looked angry for a moment and I thought he might hit me, then his face fell and he climbed out of the bed and went downstairs. I remember lying there in the dark, praying for the dawn to come.

"As soon as it gets bright," I thought to myself. "I'm throwing him out of the house once and for all."

The next day I got up early. I was waiting for him when he came downstairs.

"Get out now," I shouted at him. "Get out and don't ever darken this door again."

Oh, he put up a fight alright; blamed me, told me it was my fault, he said I drove him to it. If I had hadn't thrown him out then he wouldn't have been with the other woman. In the end, however, he left, taking his clothes and shoes with him. He knew there was no going back. I closed the front door and heaved a sigh of relief.

When I told the girls I'd thrown him out they thought I was crazy.

"Are you mad Ma? If you throw him out then she's won," said Molly referring to the other woman.

"No Molly," I said, and there was conviction in my voice, "She's done me a favour."

Once I got over the initial shock, it dawned on me that it was actually a good thing. For years I'd wanted rid of Johnny Smith and for the last two I'd been trying to throw him out, but he always persuaded me to take him back. He was an ace emotional manipulator. He knew exactly which buttons to press. But not any more; there was no way Johnny could ever manipulate me again.

Mind you he kept phoning and he tried every emotion-tugging trick in the book.

"Please take me back, please forgive me. I don't know what I was thinking. You know you've always been the only woman for me. You know I love you," he'd say and he'd ring about ten times a day and often at night when he was drunk. You'd think the years of abuse had never happened. And then on other days he'd ring and abuse me, tear me to pieces with his tongue. But it didn't affect me like it used to anymore. The tide had turned and I now had a new found strength.

Although I was glad to be free of Johnny I suddenly realised that I would to have to support myself.

"There's only one thing for it Fran," said Helen as we sat drinking tea in the kitchen one day. "You're going to have to get yourself a job."

"I know Helen but I haven't had a job for years, not since I was 15-years-old. I don't think I could do it Helen. I'm too shy," I protested.

I was completely lacking in confidence. Years of being mentally and physically abused by Johnny had worn me down and made me into a nervous wreck.

I used to walk along the street with my head bent back then and if someone said "boo" to me I'd jump. I never talked to strangers; I couldn't even look them in the eye for God's sake. I've never been a lazy person but I really thought I wasn't capable of doing any type of job, least of all something that involved dealing with the public.

At the same time I knew there was nothing else for it; I had to go looking for work. A new shopping centre had been built near my home. Helen persuaded me to go there looking for a shop job and she promised she'd help me type up a CV in her house. She even came with me.

We tried a few shops one day and eventually someone guided us towards a sandwich bar. "We don't need help at the moment," said a kindly looking woman in a kid's boutique, "but I know where they're crying out for someone to make sandwiches."

It was one job I knew I'd be well able for and as luck would have it the manageress, a young woman in her

20s, seemed like a decent sort. She took me on immediately. All I had to do was stand in the back of the shop and make sandwiches. The wages were £5 an hour and it suited me perfectly. I was pleased but terribly nervous.

"What if I slip up and get the sandwiches wrong?" I thought to myself. "What if the other staff don't like me?"

It seems ridiculous to think about now, but I had so little confidence that I questioned everything and got myself into knots over the simplest things.

Aoife agreed to look after Caitríona and I started work. I was sick with fright when I started. I felt like a school child on her first day at school but things ran smoothly. The other staff members were friendly towards me and the manageress was very patient. She trained me in and in no time I was happily smacking coleslaw and slices of ham into buttered rolls.

I didn't know myself. I remember walking home across the field, which was a shortcut to my house, after my first week of working. I'd just been given my first wages and I felt so proud of myself. That job liberated me. It made me realise that I didn't need Johnny. I, Frances Smith, could stand my own two feet and the world was my oyster.

*chapter thirty-one*

DISASTER STRUCK ONE day however. After two weeks of making sandwiches Donna called me out to the till.

"Frances I need you to work the till for me," she said. "We can't have you stuck at the back of the shop all day."

I froze. There was no way I could deal with customers; the thought terrified me. But Donna wasn't taking no for an answer.

"Come on Frances," she coaxed. "I'll train you in after work and you'll be fine. Just look straight ahead of you and key in the numbers. After a while you won't even notice the customers." I begged her to let me stay on at the sandwich counter but it was no good. The following lunchtime Donna turned to me.

"Frances we're very busy would you mind going on the till?"

My heart skipped a beat at that moment. I would sooner have jumped off Liberty Hall than gone on that till but I knew it had to be done.

At first I was shaking with fright but after half an hour I stopped noticing who the customers were and I suddenly realised I wasn't doing a bad job. What's more I was so busy I didn't even notice the people I served.

Donna smiled at me.

"I'm proud of you Fran, you're doing a great job."

For years no one had given me praise and I blushed when she said that. I felt brilliant and I loved my job. It wasn't the most glamourous of work but it meant everything to me. It started me on the road to building up my self-esteem and I'll always be grateful to Donna for the encouragement she gave me.

Things ran smoothly for a while. I felt comfortable in my new job and for the first time ever I had money to spend. It wasn't much and it only bought the basics but the point was that I, and not Johnny, controlled the finances and that was a novelty to me.

Johnny had by now moved in with his girlfriend. He still continued to phone the house on a regular basis but he didn't dare come near us anymore and even though I knew he could turn up at any moment I still felt relieved.

As it happens he did turn up but it wasn't at the house. I was standing at the till in the sandwich shop one day when the phone rang. One of the young fellas in work answered it.

"It's for you Frances," he called out. I'd already warned Donna that I was separated from my husband and that he may cause trouble.

"Put Frances on," Johnny roared down the phone.

"She's not here," said the young fella, he'd been warned that I didn't want to take calls from a man.

"She is fuckin' there, if you don't put her on I'll be waiting for you after work."

The poor lad was so scared he handed me the receiver. I took it apprehensively.

"Is that you, Fran?" he said in the old familiar voice.

"What do you want Johnny? What are you doing ringing me in work?" I said.

"That's exactly why I'm ringing," he laughed that horrible, dirty laugh of his. "I can see you."

I nearly had a heart attack on the spot. What kind of sick game was he playing now?

"What do mean? What are you talking about Johnny?" he could hear the fear in my voice and it pleased him no end.

"I'm sitting right in front of you and I can see everything."

I dropped the phone on the ground and looked around me frantically. All I could see were other shops, people with shopping bags and buggies and bright lights. The noise in the shopping centre seemed to get louder at that moment—a mixture of pop music and voices, the sound of water from a distant fountain and a general white noise typical of most modern supermarkets. My head started to spin and I felt weak.

Then I saw him, sitting a few yards away at a café table. He had a perfect view of me and he was smiling as if to say, "I've got you now".

I picked up the phone.

"Johnny, what are you doing? Would you ever leave me alone? I'm trying to work."

He laughed.

"But you shouldn't be working Frances. I've told the social welfare. They know all about you."

I turned pale as a sheet. I'd been working for three weeks by then but I'd applied for the lone parent's allowance before I got the job. I'd found out days before hand that I'd been breaking the rules, I wasn't allowed to work until I'd been accepted for the scheme and then I could do 20 hours a week. There was no way however I could give up the job then. It was Christmas and I needed every penny I could get. I was due to be accepted for the allowance any day now and I thought if I could just hang in there I might get away with it.

How Johnny found about it I have no idea, but he was always a clever one and I suppose he put two and two together. Now he'd gone and reported me to the social welfare. I was shocked but more than that I was worried.

"How on earth am I going to manage over Christmas?" I thought.

I remember standing there, crying at the till as I panicked about money.

That was a typical of Johnny. He'd do anything to hurt me. He didn't even care if his kids went hungry. That year I got £18 from the social welfare and my wages were £86 after tax. That had to do us all for Christmas. Somehow we managed. As it happens when I explained the situation to the social welfare they back-paid me after Christmas.

After that Johnny began to phone the shop on a regular basis. He'd tell them I'd stolen money from the till or nicked things. Of course I hadn't; he was trying to get me fired. Thank God for my boss Donna. She trusted me implicitly and she knew about him because I'd told her the truth. I didn't go into detail but I told her he was mad and she believed me.

"Don't worry Frances," she said. "I know you'd never steal from us."

Johnny was furious. For once he had no control over me and it killed him.

*chapter thirty-two*

DESPITE THE FACT that we were separated, Johnny continued to plague me with phone calls at all hours of the day and night. I in turn, plagued the guards to do something about him.

Most of the time he was highly abusive on the phone.

"You think you're rid of me, do you?" he'd say. "I'm not going anywhere without you, you know that? I'm going to slice you up, cut you into little ribbons before I go. I'm going to cut the gee out of you and slice off your breasts."

Sometimes I'd be physically sick after I'd put down the receiver.

The guards instructed me to put a tap on the phone and to take note of every call. I did it for a few months but he's so clever; he actually knew that the phone was tapped from the way I'd respond to his questions. If I talked too slowly he'd say, "Why are you talking like that? Is it because the phone is tapped?"

Then he'd laugh and hang up. On one occasion I was actually standing in the local garda station making a complaint about him when he rang me on the mobile. He was drunk and very belligerent.

There was female guard with me at the time and I held the phone up to her ear and let her listen to him rant. Johnny didn't have conversations; he just talked at people.

The guards always promised me they'd arrest Johnny as soon as they found him, but other than the time when I'd filed for assault the only occasion he's ever been taken into custody was one time when I was in the Mediterranean on holiday and he broke into my house.

A neighbour of mine had seen him break in and had phoned the station. They came and searched the house.

They finally found him, drunk out of his mind, hiding under the bed upstairs. He spent three weeks in prison for breaking the barring order.

He has never been arrested for threatening me since and to this day I have to wonder why. I've made hundreds of complaints to my local station. I even went to see the Superintendent on one occasion. He told me he'd look into the case for me. Still nothing was done.

Johnny Smith was never a difficult person to find. He drank in the same bar everyday and I even gave the guards the address of his new girlfriend. Still they'd say they couldn't find him. Sometimes they'd make excuses about being short staffed. Or they'd fob me off by telling me they'd arrest him the following day. I'd tell them I'd be dead the following day but it didn't seem to make a difference. Other people had been arrested for a lot less and it just didn't make sense.

In the meantime I've had to endure years of abusive phone calls, never knowing when Johnny may turn up out of the blue.

I remember one evening when I was sitting watching television with the curtains open. Caitríona was in bed and there was no one else there. Suddenly I glanced at the window and I saw a figure staring in at me. Because it was dark however I couldn't make their features. I got a terrible fright. At first I thought it was a burglar. I ran into the hall and lifted the phone to call the guards.

Then I stopped in my tracks. What would I say to them? I had to be sure there was someone out there and my imagination had not been playing tricks on me.

I tiptoed back into the sitting room and peered out into the darkness. I saw a familiar figure, hopping over the gate and running off down the road. He was wearing a long black coat that I recognised as Johnny's.

That was typical of Johnny Smith. He'd turn up to try to scare me, knowing well that I wouldn't let him into the house.

*chapter thirty-three*

JOHNNY AND MYSELF had been separated for three years when Fiona suggested that the two of us go on holiday. I had recently given up my job in the sandwich bar and I was about to start a CEO scheme. I was going to be trained as a receptionist and I was looking forward to it. In the meantime, I had a few weeks free before it started.

"Come on Frances," said Fiona while we were sitting in the kitchen. "I've found a great deal to the Mediterranean but it's next week so we'd have to act quickly."

I thought about it for all of two seconds and then I agreed. I didn't have much money at the time but I decided to get a credit union loan. It was just what I needed at the time—a holiday in the sun with no worries and away from Johnny. We booked the tickets that day and Aoife agreed to look after Caitríona.

As it happens, that holiday was the best thing that happened me in years. While I was there I met a man called Mohammad. He was slightly younger then me but very charming. Mohammad owned the bar in the hotel where we were staying and I used to see him everyday. He'd smile at me and try to make conversation, but I didn't want to talk to him.

I'd been so hurt over the years that I wanted nothing to do with any man. The only man I'd ever had a relationship with was Johnny and I presumed that all men were the same. I knocked back all of Mohammad's advances and at times I was blatantly rude to him, but unlike most Irish men he kept on trying. Over the course of the week he slowly broke me down. I began to talk to him but still I didn't trust him.

He told me he didn't drink because he was a Muslim. He claimed to be single but I didn't believe him. I was convinced he had a wife or a girlfriend and that he was lying to me.

"No my sweet," he'd say when I'd ask him, "I don't have a woman."

Funnily enough the more I shunned his advances; the more he tried to get to know me.

Fiona turned to me one night and said, "Frances, that poor man has been trying to chat you up all week and you've been horrible to him. Would you ever relax a little and go for a drink with him? If he says he's single then he must be."

I agreed to go for a drink with Mohammad. It wasn't easy for me to trust him immediately but he was a gentle, understanding man and slowly but surely we struck up a friendship. We exchanged addresses and phone numbers before I left and we promised to keep in touch.

Even then I didn't trust him completely but it was so long since any man had shown me kindness and treated me with respect that I decided to take a risk and keep in touch with him. After all we were nothing but friends so I thought there was no harm in it.

When I returned to Ireland a week later Johnny found out. Fiona and I had taken photographs in the Mediterranean and one day when I was at work, Johnny broke into the house and discovered them. He phoned me up that night.

"I found the photos," he slurred down the phone. "What are you talking about Johnny?" I said. "I found the photos, the ones of you and your toy boy."

"Oh Jesus," I thought to myself.

I knew he'd probably kill me if he thought I'd been seeing another man.

"You're my wife," he screamed down the phone, "And I forbid you to go near another man. Do you hear me?"

I put down the phone and cursed the day I ever met Johnny Smith. I continued to keep in contact with

Mohammad however and it was the start of a beautiful friendship. It killed Johnny to think of me with another man, but there was nothing he could do about it. A few days later he phoned again and as usual he was drunk.

"You know what, I've been thinking," he slurred the words. "You know I love you? Well," he hiccuped loudly down the phone. "I've decided to forgive you. I'll forget about your affair, if you let me come back. I forgive you," he sounded like the Pope and I actually laughed when I put down the receiver.

A year later I went back to the same place in the Mediterranean with Fiona. I'd kept in touch with Mohammad by post. He wrote such lovely letters and I used to look forward to receiving them. It became a pleasure to write back to him too and it gave me something to do on the long lonely, winter evenings. The odd time he'd phone and I loved to hear his voice.

Little by little I was beginning to trust this man and I realised he must be somewhat serious about me if he'd kept in touch for a whole year. The fact that he lived so far away helped matters; it was a safety valve if I ever wanted out.

I was looking forward to seeing him again and besides I needed a holiday; Johnny was tormenting me with phone calls. It didn't matter that we'd been separated for years, he'd still phone me up at all hours of the night and day. I needed to get away and forget about him for a while.

I was in great form when I got to the airport. I was standing in the middle of the departure lounge with Fiona, searching the information screen when my phone rang. It was Johnny. At first I ignored it but I knew if I didn't answer he'd keep on ringing.

"What do you want Johnny?" I gave in eventually. "I can see you," he laughed down the phone. I felt a shiver run down my back.

"What are you talking about?" I said to him.

"You're standing in the airport and I can see you," he laughed again but now I was worried.

"You thought you could go off to the Mediterranean did you?" said Johnny. "Thought you could disappear off to see that fancy man of yours, eh? Well I don't think so."

"Johnny leave me alone," I said.

"I'll not leave you alone," he said. "You're not going anywhere. I'm going to cut you into little pieces with my knife. You're not getting on that plane. I can see you and I'm coming to get you," then he laughed sadistically and hung up the phone.

I turned to Fiona.

"Was it him Frances?" she said.

The colour had drained from my face.

"It was him alright. I can't go Fiona. He's in the airport and he's going to kill me," I was shaking with the fear.

"Come on Fran," said my sister as she grabbed me by the arm and pulled me behind a pillar.

"He might not be here at all and if he is he'll have to find us."

Fiona looked at her watch.

"It's three o'clock now Fran. We've only got an hour before we board. Come on we'll hide from him."

We ran behind a pillar in the departure lounge and thought about where we could hide.

"What about the ladies' toilets?" said Fiona. "He couldn't get in there if he wanted to."

The toilets were at the other end of the lounge so we scurried off towards them as fast as we could; all the time looking around us.

"Here put these on Fran," my sister pulled a pair of sunglasses from her bag and handed them to me. They were too big for my face and I probably looked ridiculous with them on but I didn't care as long as I got on that flight before Johnny found me.

We'd just reached the toilets when the phone rang again.

"Ignore it Fran," said Fiona.

I let it go but it kept on ringing and I knew that would anger Johnny all the more.

"I'm going to answer it Fiona," I turned to my sister.

The two of us were holed up in one of the toilet cubicles by now and we were terrified. Johnny always had a knack of creeping up behind you when you least expected it. I honestly thought he might stick his head over the wall of the toilet cubicle at any moment.

"Hello?" I answered the phone trying not to sound frightened.

"So you think you're giving me the slip do you?"

It was Johnny again.

"Johnny, please, just leave me alone, please Johnny."

I started to cry then. The sound of his voice always brought tears to my eyes.

"I told you, you're not going anywhere," he said again. "I'm going to get you."

I dropped the phone on the ground. Fiona picked it up but he had gone.

"Come on Fran," she said. "We're going to get on that plane and he's not going to touch us," there was determination in her voice. The boarding gate was a ten minute walk away; it was the longest ten minutes of my life. I kept my head down and walked as fast as I could without running. I thought if I ran I would draw attention to myself.

Fiona scoured the airport. She couldn't see Johnny anywhere but the place was packed with people. It was the height of the holiday season.

"Come on Frances, we're nearly there," there was fear in her voice as she took me by the hand.

The boarding gate was just a few yards away, we could see it and as we ran towards it my heart beat faster.

"Just let me get through," I prayed. "Please God get me on to that plane alive."

I ran as fast as my legs could carry me, there was no time to look behind, all I could think about was reaching that gate. There were three people in the queue ahead of us and we waited with baited breath for them to go through, then it was our turn but just as we reached the departure entrance I felt a tap on my shoulder. My heart skipped a beat at that second and the world seemed to stand still as my mind raced. I knew what was waiting for me. I screamed.

Afterwards Fiona told me I looked as white as a sheet at that moment. I turned around and to my amazement there was a little old woman standing in front of me.

"Excuse me, I didn't mean to frighten you," she said, "but I saw you drop your passport on the ground."

She held out my passport.

By the time we got on the flight both Fiona and I were laughing hysterically. We almost expected him to be waiting for us on the plane, it didn't make sense of course but we knew Johnny was capable of anything.

We only really relaxed when we touched the ground and realised that we were hundreds of miles away from that mad man. It was only later that we figured out that Johnny probably hadn't been in the airport that day but we never knew the truth.

## *chapter thirty-four*

WHAT BEGAN AS a hesitant friendship had by now become a full-blown romance. It wasn't easy for me to trust another man but I suppose the fact that he didn't drink helped. I loved that he was consistent in the way he treated me and besides he was everything that Johnny wasn't.

Mohammad told me I was the most beautiful woman in the world. He was kind, considerate and respectful and I felt safe in his company. That was a brand new feeling for me. The only thing I could liken it to was how I'd felt when I'd first met Johnny all those years ago, but I was an innocent teenager back then. Now I was a mature woman in her 30s who had never known the love of a grown man.

Simple things like going for a drink and being able to relax were a complete novelty to me because for years I had lived in fear of Johnny and his temper.

I was a broken woman when I met Mohammad but his gentle attitude and kindness helped to restore me. I began to realise that all the doubts I had in my mind about myself were based on years of rejection and fear. He helped me to overcome them and develop a different attitude towards life. He never asked me to change and never put me down. He loved me for who I was and that feeling was a revelation to me.

When he first suggested that I move to the Mediterranean, I immediately thought, "No", I'd miss the girls too much and besides Caitríona was settled in school in Dublin and I couldn't uproot her. But as the years went on and Johnny continued to torment me with phone calls I began to give the idea serious consideration.

At one stage I decided I'd give it a go and I went to the Mediterranean for a month. While I was there I thought about how it would feel to live in that region permanently.

I imagined myself waking up to glorious sunshine all year round and listening to the chants of the Muslims as they performed their daily worship. I saw myself cooking Mediterranean meals and walking on the beach each day. Of course, I imagined myself living with Mohammad too. At that stage he had sold his bar and was now working in real estate. He made a good living from his work and we'd have a comfortable life together.

Although I will always love the Mediterranean and I have a great sense of peace in the knowledge that I am far, far away from Johnny, in the end I decided I wanted to stay in Ireland. Even though I complain about the greyness and the rain, the cost of living and the way Ireland has changed in recent years, Dublin will always be my home.

Besides I knew I'd miss my sisters and my father, I'd miss the three girls and I'd never know my grand-children. I decided Johnny Smith wouldn't stop me from living the life I chose.

Shortly after that I got a legal separation from Johnny. I remember the day it came through. I'd been to see my solicitor in the city centre and Helen had come with me.

The two of us were walking down Grafton Street afterwards. I was on a high. For years I'd dreamed of getting away from that man and now it had become a reality. I was also delighted because I finally had the house in my own name and nobody could make me leave.

It was raining that day but I didn't care; nothing could dampen my spirits. We were walking down the street, laughing and talking happily when I took off my wedding ring. It was the one Johnny had given me years ago; the one with the inscription "I Love you" on the inside.

"What are you doing Fran?" Helen was shocked.

"Sure what do I need it for now Helen?" I asked.

"It represents all those years of hardship and I don't want it," with that I lifted my arm into the air and threw it down the street with all my might. I felt like I was throwing away all those memories, all that pain and suffering. "Maybe someone else will find it and have more luck with it than I ever did."

The ring fell a few yards away and rolled down the street. I followed it with my eyes for a few seconds and then it was lost amid the footsteps of the shoppers and the rain. I smiled.

"It's a new beginning for me Helen," I said.

Ever since Caitríona had been born, Johnny had shown little interest in her. He never played with her the way he had with the other girls when they were young and to be honest he hardly knew the child. He didn't mark her birthday or buy her presents at Christmas and she didn't even call him Da.

The only man she had ever known was Mohammad and he had been more of a father to her than Johnny. She knew that Johnny existed and I never said anything bad about him in her company.

Once we separated however he started asking if he could see her. Unlike the other girls Caitríona had grown up with no memory of the years of abuse. As a result her childhood had been happy and carefree. I wanted to keep it that way.

It did worry me however that she had no father and I didn't want her to turn on me years later and blame me for never knowing her father, so I agreed.

Johnny wanted to take her out every Sunday afternoon. The only way I could let her go was if I accompanied them. I didn't trust that man. I knew he was capable of anything and I wanted to protect my daughter at all costs. Caitríona had become a great favourite with all of us. The three girls were all mad about her, as were Helen and Fiona.

One Sunday afternoon the three of us we went to dinner. Johnny brought to us a posh restaurant in town and paid for the meal by credit card. Caitríona was only eight at the time and it meant nothing to her really. She sat between us, ate ice cream and smiled shyly at Johnny.

I found it strange to play Daddies and Mammies with my ex-husband. Stranger still was the way he treated me—as if I was the love of his life. All through the meal he begged me to take him back.

"Please," he said. "Please take me back. You know you're the only woman for me? Nobody else matters."

I actually found it comical, up to a point. Ever since I'd found out about the affair Johnny knew there was no way I'd ever take him back and that just made him want me all the more. You'd think the years of abuse had never happened and he continued to ring me everyday. It drove me mad and I longed for the day he would leave me alone.

Shortly after that, I was awarded full custody of Caitríona. Legally Johnny didn't have a leg to stand on. He'd been unemployed for years and I'd got five barring orders against him, besides he didn't even show up at the court on the day. Mind you he was furious when he found out. I knew he didn't care about Caitríona, but he just wanted to use her as a way of getting at me.

Before that he had been threatening to kidnap her.

"I'm going to snatch her as she comes out of school," he used to say to me on the phone. "She's my daughter and she belongs to me. I'm going to take her and you're never going to see her again."

I was terrified. I knew Johnny Smith was capable of anything and I loved that child so much I couldn't bear for her to be hurt.

On one occasion I was going to the Mediterranean for a holiday, Caitríona was eight-years-old and I'd decided it was time she came with me. I booked the tickets and then I realised I'd need Johnny's permission to bring her. I rang the passport office and they told me I needed to notify my husband 21 days in advance of my trip. I didn't have 21 days so I would have to get a court order to bring her out of the country. Of course Johnny challenged it and I knew if we went court he'd bring up the fact that I had a boyfriend in the Mediterranean.

I worried myself sick for two weeks and then two days before we were due to go, we were called to the court.

Johnny seemed confident as he stood up in front of the judge that day.

"Your honour," he said in his best accent. "My wife," and he pointed at me, "is taking my baby abroad on holiday. She's going to the Mediterranean to see her boyfriend."

He made reference to his "baby" a number of times before the judge interrupted him.

"Excuse me Mr. Smith," he said, "but what age is 'your baby'?"

"She's eight your honour," said Johnny.

The judge replied, "Well I don't think she's a baby, do you Mr. Smith?"

"No your honour," said Johnny and he hung his head. I could tell he was afraid of the judge. Johnny always had a fear of the law.

Then the judge turned to me.

"Is this true Mrs. Smith? Do you intend to visit your boyfriend in the Mediterranean?"

My heart was racing as I answered him. I felt guilty even though I'd done nothing wrong. I felt as if I had no right to have a boyfriend, but there no way out of it. I looked the judge in the eye and held my head high.

"Yes your honour," I replied. "We'll be staying in his apartment."

"And do you plan to return to Ireland?" asked the judge.

"Of course your honour," I replied.

Suddenly Johnny stood up in the courtroom and shouted at the judge.

"I want it stipulated that my wife will return to Ireland with my baby," he said.

Up to now Johnny had been on his best behaviour but now he was making a fool of himself. The judge turned to him and it was obvious that he was annoyed.

"Please sit down Mr. Smith."

Johnny did as he was told but he was angry. I knew he felt foolish. Then the judge spoke again.

"What part of what I've told you do you not understand? This woman is not your 'wife'," he said pointing at me.

"And the child is not a baby. She's eight-years-old."

Then he asked Johnny if he was presently supporting "the baby" and Johnny said, "No", he was unemployed.

The judge turned to me.

"I'm putting that child on your passport until she's 18-years-old Mrs. Smith," he said. "So you won't have to come back in here again."

I was delighted. Johnny sat there with his head bent and when he did look up he was furious.

"And Mrs. Smith," said the judge before we finished, "I hope you have a great holiday because you deserve it."

Then he turned to Johnny.

"By the way Mr. Smith, that child will return when your ex-wife decides to bring her back."

I walked out of the courtroom on air. For once I had won the battle and there was nothing Johnny Smith could do about it. Caitríona and I went off two days later and I never enjoyed a holiday more.

*chapter thirty-five*

ALL THE GIRLS had continued to keep in touch with their father despite the fact that we were separated. When Johnny and I first split up, I thought that they would cut off all contact with him like I was trying to do, but they didn't and it upset me.

I couldn't understand why they would pass the time of day with him after everything we'd been through over the years.

Despite everything that had happened they still felt sorry for him. They used to call in to see him every now and then, or if he came to visit their flats they wouldn't turn him away. Johnny knew how to manipulate them and they were confused.

On the one hand, they felt angry and on the other, they felt a loyalty to him because he was their father.

On one occasion Johnny called around to the house. Molly was visiting me at the time with her baby who was just six-months old.

Johnny was drunk and abusive as he always was after one too many drinks. He began to verbally abuse poor Molly for no reason whatsoever. She was in the back bedroom at the time and her baby was lying in the centre of the bed. Johnny got so angry that he started to thump the bed with his fist and the baby flew up in the air each time he hit it.

Molly was distraught. She took a run at him and landed on top of her father on the bed. Then she started punching him in the face, just like he'd punched her for all those years. She'd had a good teacher. She knew exactly when to pull back her arm and how to aim for his jaw or his eye socket.

"Leave my baby alone you bastard," she screamed at the top of her voice. "It's over now," she sobbed as she punched his face with all her might—again and again and again, until he was crying like a pathetic child.

"It's over," she shouted and there was deep-seethed anger in her voice. "You can't hurt me anymore."

By the time she'd finished Johnny's face was covered in bruises and he had cuts all over it too. But more than anything his pride was hurt.

The trouble didn't end there however. Keith, Molly's boyfriend, was never one to take things lying down and he was furious when he'd heard what had happened.

"That bastard, Molly," he said. "I'm going to show him."

Before Molly could stop him Keith grabbed a hammer from the back garden and drove off to find Johnny who had sought refuge in the pub.

I got a phone call from Molly as soon as he had left.

"Oh Ma," she sobbed. "What are we going to do? Keith's going to kill Da. I know it."

I literally didn't know what to do. Part of me wanted Johnny to die and the other part was thinking of Molly and how guilty she'd feel for the rest of her life and that broke my heart. I phoned for an ambulance and gave them the address of Johnny's girlfriend.

Keith returned an hour later, he was fuming with rage and there was blood all over the hammer. As it happens Johnny didn't die that night but he received 170 stitches in his head. Keith had stormed into the pub and attacked him with the hammer. He'd beaten him over the head continuously. It's a wonder he wasn't brain damaged for life.

Johnny phoned Molly when they released him from the hospital.

"If you stay with that man I'll disown you," he shouted down the phone.

Of course, Molly had no intention of leaving Keith and Johnny didn't speak to her for four months after that. Eventually he gave in and to this day he has never raised a hand to her. He knows better now because she has a man who will stand up for her and Johnny Smith is really just a coward.

A few months after however he picked on poor Aoife who has always been a softie. She'd forgiven him more times than I can remember. He called around to her flat one day looking for a lift to the pub.

"I have to meet a mate," he said to her, "and I need a lift urgently.

"I'm sorry Da, I can't," said Aoife, who was six-months pregnant at the time. "I'm not feeling well today."

Like that he had punched her in the face and she fell to the floor with the impact. It didn't matter that Aoife was now a woman who was expecting his grandchild.

Johnny didn't care and he never apologised. Luckily the baby was okay and a few months later I had another grandson.

The irony is that she was actually hurt that Johnny never came to the hospital to see the new baby.

"You'd have thought he'd want to see his own grandson," she said to me afterwards but then Aoife has never been one to hold grudges.

I worry about her but then I worry about each and every one of my girls in different ways. I know the scars they have cannot be seen on the outside and I fear that what they have been through will affect their own relationships in years to come.

Molly did a self-assertiveness course a while ago and she felt all the better for it. I was proud of her of course but I would love all of them to go to counselling because I think it might help them to stand up to Johnny.

*chapter thirty-six*

ONE DAY MOHAMMAD phoned me unexpectedly from the Mediterranean. "Hello Frances," he said in his warm accent. "How are you doing my sweet? Frances, I'm thinking of coming to Ireland for a few weeks to see you. What do you think? Is it a good idea or not?"

I was so pleased that he wanted to come over that of course I encouraged him. I hadn't seen him for a few months and I missed him. But as soon as I put down the phone I began to worry. What would Johnny do if he found out?

Johnny had been living with Sarah ever since we separated, they were now considered a couple and were regularly seen about town together.

Despite the fact that he had a girlfriend, he still continued to plague me with phone calls and I never knew when he might turn up to the house.

I decided however to take a risk and invite Mohammad over. I had been the recipient of his hospitality for years and I wanted to repay him. Besides I thought, "Why should I let Johnny ruin my relationship? He controlled my life for 22 years and that's enough."

Helen came with me to the airport on the day that he arrived. The two of us had planned out an itinerary for his three-week stay. We wanted him to enjoy himself.

The three weeks passed all too quickly. It was the summer time and I took him to see all the sights of Dublin. We visited Trinity College, Christ Church and the art galleries. He took me out to dinner in nice restaurants and we drank in bars in the city centre.

I couldn't relax however. I was constantly looking over my shoulder to see if Johnny happened to be walking up the road. Many a time I was convinced I'd seen him and I made Mohammad duck behind a wall or stand in a doorway until I was sure the coast was clear. I knew word had got out that Mohammad was visiting me and I was sure he would be looking for us about Dublin; that was Johnny's style. What's more I knew for certain that he'd kill both of us if we encountered him.

My lover tried to calm me down. "Don't be worrying Frances, my little flower," he used to say and I'd still blush when he gave me compliments.

In the end we got away without meeting Johnny. Looking back I'm convinced he was scared; he didn't want to meet another man—a man who would stand up to him and probably be able for him. Johnny only ever took on those he knew to be weaker than him.

At this stage, I have resigned myself to living in Dublin with or without Mohammad. The best I can do is try to see him a couple of times a year and live in the knowledge that there is man out there who loves me for who I am and will never cause me to fear him.

*chapter thirty-seven*

TO THIS DAY the blood runs to my toes whenever I see a man with grey hair on the street. When I first met Johnny he had striking jet-black hair, but he's older now and it's long ago turned grey. He was a different person back then and so was I.

Mind you I'm a lot better than I was. People tell me I look ten years younger than I used to. I colour my hair now and wear a bit of make-up. I look after my skin and wear pretty clothes. I take pride in myself.

I still live in the same house and I now work as a receptionist but I have more freedom than I used to. I can now make plans to go on holiday or meet my sisters for a drink. I can go for a walk in the sunshine if I feel like it. I have a life, but I'm always looking over my shoulder.

I still don't sleep properly at night because the fear is always there. I know Johnny so well that I wouldn't put anything past him. I know now that if I were to move to some other part of Dublin, or Ireland for that matter, he'd find out where I was and make life hell for me.

Johnny is an obsessive character and I am his obsession. My only hope is that one day he'll be locked up. Besides all the pain and suffering he has put me through, he is an out-and-out criminal and he's stolen more money in his lifetime than you or I could imagine.

He phoned me up a few months ago. "I'm in spot of bother," he said as if we were the best of friends. "I need somewhere to stay for a few days. Do you think I could stay in the house?" he begged me. "Please I'll give you £300 and a leather jacket."

I put down the phone and laughed. Then I cried.

I try to laugh about him all the time; make light of the years of suffering and pretend it doesn't hurt. The girls and I joke about Johnny amongst ourselves, we have to do it to stay sane; it's our way of coping. But the truth is the pain is always there and I fear it always will be.

It was my birthday a few months ago and he phoned me. "How are you?" he asked like he'd seen me the week before. "I miss you," his voice trailed off with emotion. "I know it's your birthday, Fran, I've been thinking; would you like to come out with me for a date? I'll take you somewhere nice and buy you something pretty to wear, what do you think, Fran, will you come? You know you're the love of my life?" he said. "You've always been the only woman for me."

It didn't matter that we were legally divorced at this stage and had been for the last five years, in Johnny's eyes I will be his until the day that I die. He actually told the girls recently that I was going through a "mad phase" and that sooner or later I'd let him come back.

Although I still live in fear of him, the truth has set me free and I am a different person because of it. I used to think that I was the only battered wife in the country. I knew other women had abusive husbands but I honestly thought that no situation was as bad as mine. It's only in recent years and from talking about Johnny to other people that I've discovered the other horror stories out there.

To those who have never experienced abuse my story must sound unbelievable. But believe me no woman is immune. They say that one in five in Irish women are battered wives.

What's more it's a phenomenon, which crosses every race and class boundary. That stranger on the bus who doesn't look you in the eye, that woman who works alongside you in the office, the lady who serves you in your local newsagents or your friend or even your sister, could all be battered wives.

It is now I realise that it is our silent suffering, which allows the victimisation to continue. And although the physical scars heal it is the mental torture, which leaves the deepest wound, a wound which is only truly understood by those who have lived through it.

I would hope that in some small way this story may help those who have been or who are battered wives and who know what it is like to live in daily fear as I did. Believe me, there is hope. If I can make a new life, then so can you.